CONTEN

FOREWORD

When I wrote the German original of this book one year ago, it was my aim to give a true picture of the status of our dogs – man's best friends – at the end of the 20th century. It is a matter of fact that the conditions for dog-keeping have changed dramatically during the last 50 years. I wonder how much longer dog lovers and public opinion will tolerate the fact that quite a number of Breed Standards do not consider, carefully and in a responsible way, the health of the dogs.

At dog shows, we meet canine giants and dwarfs – both are unsound as regards their anatomy. In quite a few breeds there are genetically-linked diseases which are good news for vets, but less attractive for the owners of these dogs. I personally think that the Breed Standards for each dog breed throughout the world must be seriously controlled if interpretations of them are leading to anatomical exaggerations. Yes, this has been declared as an aim by kennel clubs all over the world again and again, but I have been heavily involved on the international dog scene for more than 40 years and, so far, there have been only tiny moderations of Standards with regard to health problems and the longevity of our dogs.

The main problem we face today is a considerably altered public attitude towards dogs and dog-keeping. The majority of the population still loves 'Lassie' Collies, 'Beethoven' St Bernards, 101 Dalmatians (in the movies) or Bobtails and Basset Hounds (in the ads), but are dog lovers really prepared to deal with the problems connected with ownership of dogs nowadays? What is the life of modern dogs in our

big cities like, in reality? What are we to do with our dogs
during all the holidays which punctuate our working lives?
Where do we find people who are educating their dogs
properly, so that there are no problems with neighbours over
barking, growling and fouling parks and streets? There is no
doubt that it takes a lot of time and money these days to
keep a dog in our modern communities, in crowded streets
with a huge volume of traffic. The very aggressive anti-dog
lobby is seriously claiming that, in bigger towns, there
should be no dogs at all. Animal shelters are overcrowded
with unwanted dogs. Dogs bought as Christmas presents for
children are dispatched four weeks later to shelters or to rescue rescue organisations.

Aibo, the new computerised robot dog developed by Sony,
seems to offer a real alternative to a living animal. You can
play with Aibo; he can bark, move, chase a red ball, and,
afterwards, you can simply put him in a corner of the room.
There is no need to feed him, to take him to the vet or to
walk him out in the rain. He can patiently wait a long time
until his master is in the mood to play with him again. Is
Aibo, in our modern world, the right dog for the new generation?

In this book, I have tried to demonstrate how important
our dogs are in 2001, in this new century and new millennium. What are our children without real dogs; so patient, so
happy and true partners and friends for them? They offer
their lifetime's devotion to the child. What is a family without a dog, the last link to nature? What a dramatic source of
help are our dogs for the blind, deaf and disabled or elderly
people living alone! How important are dogs to the police,
and to rescue teams searching for lost humans? How important are dogs searching for explosives and drugs? This is a
very long list of reason that prove how urgently we need
dogs in our lives.

This book sets out to demonstrate that a sensible and long-
term public relations campaign is important, in order to
guarantee broad social acceptance of dogs in all our communities. We must show the media, day by day, what dogs
are doing for their owners, and how much more pleasant
human life is if a dog is part of the family. It must become

the most important goal of all kennel and breed clubs in the world to strengthen public acceptance and tolerance of people who love their dogs.

One year ago, of course, I knew that living with dogs in the new century would certainly become more difficult, but even in my worst dreams I could not foresee what was to happen in the aftermath of one sad day in June 2000, when a six-year-old boy in Hamburg was killed in a Pitbull attack. Yes, this accident really was a nightmare for anyone with any feelings, but it was proven that the owner of the dog was a criminal who had trained his Pitbull to bite. The local authorities and police actually knew that this dog was 'trained' by his master in the schoolyard where the dreadful accident happened some time later. The authorities had ordered that the dog must always be kept muzzled and leashed, but, unfortunately, nobody ever checked whether this order was obeyed. After the attack, it was proven that the Pitbull had not been fed for several days – his stomach contained nothing but drugs. It was a very sad accident, caused by the completely criminal owner of a sadly abused dog.

Nobody could have predicted what would happen in the days after this attack. Huge newspaper headlines asked what politicians had done to protect people from these 'killer dogs'. Every television station reported the accident and shocked people by alleging that similar accidents could easily happen in any German town.

Everybody knows what happens when the mass media are causing hysteria – almost the whole of the German nation was in shock and fear of 'fighting dogs' which were (apparently) strolling uncontrolled through our big and small towns, looking for new prey.

Politicians knew that this sad accident in Hamburg would not have happened if the local police had enforced the official order to keep this particular Pitbull on leash and muzzle. But, backed by the mass media and accused of having done nothing to protect the health and security of their citizens, these politicians swore to free German towns from 'fighting dogs' in the near future.

Here are some examples of what they said:

Gerhard Schroeder (German chancellor), June 28th 2000:
"These fighting machines must get off the streets."

Orrwin Runde (Mayor of Hamburg), June 27th 2000:
"We don't need such dogs! They are nothing other than weapons, instruments of war."

Doris Schroeder-Koepf (wife of the German chancellor), June 29th 2000:
"Freedom for children or freedom for fighting dogs? Germany must make the right choice."

Orrwin Runde, June 29th 2000:
"Our aim is to euthanase as many dogs as possible! This is very difficult to understand for lovers of animals and dogs, but our absolute priority is to protect people... It can be predicted now that in the future there will be no more fighting dogs in Hamburg."

Viktor Bouffier (Minister of Internal Affairs in Hessen), June 29th 2000:
"All these fighting machines have to vanish out of our country."

Otto Schily (Federal Minister of Internal Affairs), July 1st 2000):
"We do not accept that health and life of humans should be endangered by the aggression and missing responsibility of certain dog owners."

It is a sad fact that all these German politicians were not talking only about Pitbulls – in Category One of the new anti-dog decree, which includes the most 'dangerous' breeds, they have placed Pitbulls, American Staffordshire Terriers, Bull Terriers and Staffordshire Bull Terriers. And, just to show how ridiculous this breed list is, all the German breeds like the German Shepherd, Dobermann and Rottweiler are not regarded as dangerous to our population.

All dog experts and behaviourists worldwide agree that it is not possible to ban an entire breed for being dangerous. The real danger is always the individual dog owner, who abuses a single dog. These facts have been documented and dog experts have presented them to parliaments and governments, but nobody in Germany was interested, either in these facts or in the statistics on biting incidents, which prove that most accidents involving dogs were caused by German Shepherds and crossbreeds. In my opinion, Germany is not governed by responsible politicians any longer, only by hysteria and the headlines of the yellow press.

It would be wrong to think that only the few breeds mentioned above, and their owners, have suffered from the new legislation. Germany is a federation of sixteen single states or 'lands', and each made up its own breed list. The most stringent regulations can be found in North Rhine-Westphalia (NRW), where the list of 'dangerous breeds' in Category One covers thirteen 'breeds' including Pitbulls, American Staffordshire Terriers, Staffordshire Bull Terriers, Bull Terriers, the Neapolitan Mastiff, the Mastin Español, the Dogue de Bordeaux, the Dogo Argentino, the Fila Brasileiro, the Tosa Inu and (a curiosity) the Bandog, and all crosses of these breeds! In Category Two, 29 other breeds are included, for instance the Bullmastiff, the Mastiff, the Tibetan Mastiff, the Briard, and, very suprisingly, the Rottweiler and the Dobermann, the only two breeds of German origin.

Dogs in Category One must always be muzzled and kept on a leash in public areas. It is strictly forbidden to breed or import these dogs. Every single animal must be castrated or spayed. The individual owner and his dog are strictly licensed and controlled. The dog must undergo a special behaviour test, and if it shows signs of aggressiveness, it is taken away. The owner has to prove that he has complete control over his dog in every situation and that he has the necessary knowledge to handle such a dog.

If a dog seems to be aggressive in the test or if the owner does not meet the above requirements, the dogs are taken to an animal shelter or euthanased. In cities like Hamburg and Berlin, so-called dog prisons exist, and most authorities agree that, if the confiscated dogs do not find a new owner within four weeks, they will be euthanased too. But who wants a dog which is stigmatized in the eyes of the public? All these tests and personal controls are to be paid for by the dog's new owner, who is also charged for the veterinary costs of neutering the dog. Moreover, the so-called 'Kampfhundesteuer' is waiting for the new owner – many towns or villages are imposing an annual dog tax for each 'fighting dog' and this can be as much as DM 1,200.

If you compare these German regulations to the UK's stupid 'Dangerous Dogs Act', you will see how lucky British dog owners still are. However, you must be clearly aware of the fact that the German government will endeavour to do everything possible in Brussels to spread this German legislation to all EC countries, in order to ban all 'fighting dogs'. Don't be so sure that these efforts will fail! There are quite a few other European countries who already have their own anti-dog legislation; for instance, France, the Netherlands and Belgium. What a lot of nonsense has already been agreed upon in Brussels!

The German anti-dog legislation is the biggest success so far of the 'anti-dog lobby' worldwide. Hundreds and thousands of dogs and their owners are suffering, and nobody can really answer the question as to what will happen in the future. The outlook is very gloomy!

You must also be fully aware that campaigns, such as those taking place in Germany, are doing damage to all breeds and to all dog owners. There have already been serious physical attacks on blind and disabled people and their dogs. They have been insulted and accused of having guide dogs that are a danger to children and old people. Dogs have been attacked by hooligans and some really cruel incidents have happened; for example, petrol was poured over a dog which was then set on fire. Hundreds of dogs have been poisoned by unfriendly neighbours and rogues. Many German dog owners prefer, nowadays, to walk their dogs at night in order to avoid assaults.

Even the English proverb 'My home is my castle' is no longer true. Landlords and large building societies are asking their tenants the question: 'What is more valuable to you, your dog or your home?' Often, neighbours go to landlords complaining that they and their children do not feel safe any longer if a dog is allowed to be kept in the same house. Children who have played with friendly dogs for years are no longer allowed to do so by their parents. Anti-dog hysteria is growing and growing!

These were the very sad, but very true, facts in Germany during the year 2000. Do you understand now how important it is to think seriously about *Quo Vadis Canis?* or *The Dog, an endangered species?*

I cannot promise you an amusing book, but, rather, some very serious facts and a vision of what might happen in the future if all dog lovers do not start to co-operate, to protect man's best friend and to impress upon the general public how important dogs are to all of us – now and for the next hundred years!

Dr Dieter Fleig

Chapter One
A SUITABLE CASE FOR PROTECTION

What do our pet dogs have in common with an ostrich? You'll never guess! The Federal Chamber of Veterinarians in Bonn, Germany proclaimed the ostrich as the 1995 Species for Animal Protection. In 1996, this organisation protested in a similar way against Man's treatment of his oldest household companion – the dog.

VETERINARY CONCERNS
Germany's Federal Chamber of Veterinarians is a central organisation consisting of 28,000 veterinarians, who are affiliated with the organisation through their local veterinary chapters. The combined knowledge of national veterinary medicine is united at this nerve centre. The adoption of the dog as a 'Species for Animal Protection' is a reflection of the everyday life of every veterinarian.

The veterinarians' criticism was directed at "ambitious breeding, exotic breeding, ignorance and professed ignorance that has led to so-called 'Qualzucht'" (breeds that suffer due to the extreme physical standards set by dog breeders).

The goal of the Federal Chamber of Veterinarians is not to eliminate purebred dogs, but to protect them from pain, suffering and long-term breed-orientated physical deficiencies.

BREED-SPECIFIC PROBLEMS
Professor Dr Alexander Herzog, geneticist at the University

of Glessen, has declared war on 'Qualzucht' breeding that causes undue suffering in certain breeds of dog. He maintains that "certain breed-orientated physical goals (form, colour, performance, behaviour) lead to underachievement in growth, immunity, maintenance and reproduction". He specifically stresses that not only anatomical, but also behavioural, abnormalities have developed. Professor Herzog names "growth (giants and Toys); fur and skin quality (Mexican Hairless); the merle factor; overly exaggerated wrinkles (Shar Pei); skull shape (short muzzle, pug-like head); and eyes (protruding eyes)".

Dr Jürgen Arndt, specialist in small animals, points out with regret that certain typical illnesses often seem to occur in the same breed of dog. This happens, not only in exotic canines, like the Mexican Hairless or the Shar Pei, but also in well-known miniature breeds such as the Yorkshire Terrier and the Pekingese. What's more, two of the breeds most popular with dog owners over the years – the German Shepherd and the Dachshund – also suffer from specific diseases.

The Chamber noted that they were not just singling out 'exotics', but that many well-known breeds are also affected. For example, extreme Toy dog types with paper-thin, sensitive skulls, and extremely short-muzzled canine types with whelping difficulties and chronic breathing problems were listed too. Certain breeds have even developed their own particular diseases (e.g.'Teckellähme' or rear-leg paralysis). The dogs are suffering, not because they belong to a certain breed, but because the Standard for that breed has become progressively more extreme (for example, larger or smaller).

The organisation even went so far as to suggest that certain Breed Standards be officially banned. Professor Dr Herzog concludes: "The highest commandment should be: Those individuals who, through their activity as breeders, damage life forms must fully realise that they can be held accountable in a court of law for their actions supporting cruelty to animals. This directive is also meant for, though not only intended for, canine breeding practices!"

Dr Arndt selected examples from his small-animal clinic's medical file. Over the past few decades, two of the most popular canine breeds particularly prone to developing special diseases were:

1. The German Shepherd: HD (Hip Disorder Syndrome); Myasthenia gravis (nerve/muscle disease); backbone disc disorders (German Shepherd paralysis); kidney stones; bloat.
2. The Dachshund: Teckellähme (rear-leg paralysis); kidney disease (Cushing Syndrome); eye disease; nerve disease (epilepsy, narcolepsy).

Small canine breeds are particularly popular because they are easier to maintain. Dr Arndt selects the following breeds and their potential problems:

Yorkshire Terrier (brain and heart disease)

Pekingese (brain, backbone disc, eye disease)

Maltese (slipped disc, eye disease)

Chihuahua (hydrocephalus, idiopathic aortanstenosis, spina bifida (spinal growth deficiency), diabetes, heart disease, patellar luxation)

The above is just a short excerpt from this cry for help from a veterinary organisation intent on saving our canines from their own breeders. There are also positive accompanying words, suggesting that the various dog breeding clubs should actively support the findings of the Federal Chamber of Veterinarians by working together with genealogists and, when necessary, modifying Standards in favour of dogs. It was proposed that all breeds considered in the category of 'Qualzucht' should be banned from dog shows.

HAS ANYTHING CHANGED?

The ripples of disquiet that followed the action taken in 1996 have all but disappeared. I personally don't think that anything has appreciably changed. Which causes me to recollect that in 1987, nine years before the Chamber of Veterinarians' desperate cry for help, I presented my newly published book *The Technique of Canine Breeding* to an audience of professionals in the Maximum Auditorium of the University of Vienna. This book called for a completely new set of priorities in canine breeding. My priorities were then as they are today: Health, Intelligence, Performance and, only then, Beauty!

My demands were greeted with general agreement, support, and brought words of praise. Even back then, I suggested that all Breed Standards be reviewed to determine which regulations were responsible for the resulting health deficiencies. Within the FCI (Fédération Cynologique Internationale), the world's foremost canine breeders' association, a committee was formed to rewrite a new set of Breed Standards. This committee worked diligently for several years, and the results remind me of the proverb of the mountain that moved – and gave birth to a mouse. Nothing had changed. Breed Standards overall remained the same, in accordance with the honourable tradition of each individual breed.

Perhaps it should additionally be noted that, from this book's point of view, the perspective of the Federal Chamber of Veterinarians was too focused on purebred canine breeding and the resulting health deficiencies. The real problem lies very much deeper, and touches all aspects of our own social and economic life. At this point, I would like to postpone this topic until Chapter Three in which my co-author Stig Carlson will discuss *The Dog, Man's Best Friend – even in the Third Millennium?*

Chapter Two
ROBOT DOGS TAKE A BOW-WOW

Are you a computer freak and also a dog lover? Then you'll certainly be interested in a brand-new invention – the Robo Dog. In the United States, the Japanese electronics company Sony recently let off the leash an artificially intelligent robot dog. The first 2,000 were sold out over the Internet within a week at the hefty price of $2,450. Demand is enormous and collectors' prices have already risen to between $3,200 and $4,100! Sony, a global conglomerate, possesses an excellent marketing strategy that will be, from the way things have started, extremely successful. The computerised canine even has his own name, AIBO, which means 'partner' in Japanese.

AIBO – THE PUSH-BUTTON PET
AIBO reacts to the world around him, learns his own tricks, expresses emotions – just like a real dog – but only when you push the 'on' button. He is the ultimate fantasy for those dog owners who have already grown tired of taking care of their household pet.

AIBO barks, walks, scratches imaginary fleas – what's more, he doesn't have to be fed, brushed or taken for a walk. This fine piece of precision-made computer technology only weighs 1,588 grams (about 3 or 4 lbs).

AIBO doesn't have fur, hunger or a circulatory system, but, even so, he can express emotions; happiness or sadness are conveyed by emitting sounds and changing the colour of his eyes. Red eyes mean anger and green eyes mean happiness. If you program him to make noises, he can bark. And this little canine robot isn't even as big as a Chihuahua – about 11 ins (28 cms) high. That's about the right relationship to the size of his 'computer brain' that allows him to move like a real, live dog. He is his inventors' 'dream come true' – pure entertainment and, of course, a great economic success.

Just like a genuine canine, AIBO has four legs, a tail and a cold nose. He sees through a 180,000 pixel camera that is carried in his nose. He hears through a microphone in his ears and barks through a little speaker in his mouth. His brain is driven by a computer – a 100-Mhz, 64-bit RISC-processor with a 16MB memory bank. Through sensors and various programs he can learn, and react to the world around him.

Once you flip the switch, AIBO can bark, go for a walk, sit down, lie down, scratch himself, etc. But these feats don't happen naturally. Somehow, you get the feeling that things keep repeating themselves... AIBO can, however, learn much more. If he runs into a wall, then he can 'figure out' not to do it again.

If you own a PC, then you can program new commands into AIBO's brain by using a memory stick, installed for that purpose under his tail. What a fantastic idea for a dog train-er who happens to be having problems training his pet!

MORE ARTIFICIAL ANIMALS

By this time, you've probably already guessed that the com-puter industry has planned additional pet models for manu-facture, on the assumption that AIBO proves to be a success. Cats, chickens and rabbits are pencilled in for production. Anyone who has studied or is familiar with the enormous selection of Tamagotchi children's toys available on the mar-ket has surely recognised that this sector of the industry knows how to make a profit. Japan, home of the Tamagotchi, replaces animals with computers and believes that the world is better because of it!

At any rate, Sony invested five years of research into devel-oping AIBO. Anatomically, the cyber-pet has 18 joints. He can lift his leg and you hear the sound of running water, but everything stays dry. He has distance sensors in his eyes. A bright pink colour activates the sensors, causing him to fol-low the colour. If you throw a pink ball, AIBO will follow it – but only at a speed of about five metres per minute. He chases the luminous pink colour, not the ball itself.

Sony believes that AIBO will find only a limited number of admirers, and that they will be the kind of person who is a computer freak and, at the same time, a dog lover. The big advantage is, of course, that AIBO never has to be taken out for a walk, nor does he demand to be fed if you happen to come home from work tired. He doesn't shed his hair or have to have his claws trimmed. He never chases squirrels – that is, unless they're hot pink!

For the moment, AIBO is still an oddity, a robot game for cyber freaks. For me, it is depressing to imagine that one day such a computerised canine could become a substitute for a real dog!

HAS THE REAL DOG HAD HIS DAY?

Ask yourself these questions and answer honestly! What would you do with a real dog during your vacation? What if the dog doesn't want to be left alone while you are at work? Will you have to walk the dog every day, even in the worst kind of weather? And how about the trouble you may have with the neighbours?

Recently, I was shocked after speaking to some senior citizens who had always shared their life with a dog. Shortly before their retirement, I began hearing statements like, "When we finally retire, we would like to travel quite a bit. We certainly won't get another dog, because a dog would restrict our personal freedom and would only cause problems".

Many people now suffer daily restrictions involved in owning a dog, which is a result of being a member of the kind of mass society we belong to.

In the future, could AIBO be (in a progressive, refined version) a product geared to an enormous household market? Does this computer conglomerate plan to provide a product just for a market of techno freaks, or have they assumed that, because of environmental conditions which make people in our society more and more hostile towards dogs, that certain individuals would prefer to own a pet robot that one can turn off or on at will?

Let's make one thing clear. Robots cannot replace living animals. They can only imitate them. Who would want to cuddle a robot? Where are the feelings in these artificial objects? Do you remember the terrible Tamagotchi hysteria in our children's bedrooms? This 'animal substitute' was dragged into classrooms by the children themselves, so that they 'could feel good'. The phenomenon was a convincing example of how children urgently need animals, and also a pitiful demonstration of what we can actually offer them at the turn of the 21st century.

We must recognise that we too are experiencing difficult times as animal breeders. Think of Dolly, the cloned sheep. Think of the mammoth that was examined first and foremost to determine whether it could be cloned and exist in our world! Are these the prospects facing us in the third millenium? Next, let's see what Stig Carlson has to say.

Chapter Three

THE DOG: A MAN'S BEST FRIEND – EVEN IN THE THIRD MILLENIUM?

by Stig G. Carlson

Members of the canine species have now padded into the third millennium, taking with them at least 20,000 years of shared history with Homo sapiens. They were scarcely aware of the turn of the millennium (neither is more than half of the Earth's human population). Though dogs, cats and bears originate from the same animal, canines alone have played a unique role in the development (for want of a more modest word) of Mankind. The dog has not only been the 'friend' of humans, as the cat is in our modern world; it has been a crucial component in the formation of the structure of our human society. Dogs, in almost any shape and form, have followed us and performed dozens of tasks for us; from being an early warning instrument and cleaning agent (in their early, semi-domesticated relationship with Man) to the highly advanced functions they perform today.

The almost absurd paradox is that, as we march ahead into the 21st century, dogs are still providing indispensable services: as health-promoting family members, as guide dogs, as the most effective mine-sweeping agents on earth, as service dogs to the handicapped, as guardians against the smuggling of toxic substances, as sporting companions, as life-extending partners in paediatric and geriatric care – and all this, believe it or not, as an endangered species!

THE SEVEN THREATS AGAINST DOGS

There are many ways of measuring our appreciation of dogs in today's world. Declining registration numbers in many kennel clubs tell their own tale. Stagnating numbers of entries in dog sports events are a reality. Consumer attitude surveys indicate that human interests are taking new and different forms. Sensationalist journalism, antagonistic to dogs, is more and more commonplace (unfortunately, some of the subjects are undeniable and of real concern). And, above all, hostile anti-canine legislative proposals, as well as currently established laws and regulations, suggest that the future of domestic dogs is much more at risk than we have dared to think.

I can identify at least seven reasons for this risk. No doubt some of these threats will accelerate during the years to come.

1. The explosion of new leisure-time activities, many of which have been classified as 'sports'.

Hobbies such as beach volleyball would hardly have been seen as 'sports' even a decade ago. But the increasing amount of time available for personal activities has created new hobbies at a mind-boggling pace (and with equally mind-boggling technology – just take a look at a pair of advanced rollerblades). Today's youth has a never-ending list of choices for both indoor and outdoor activities. Neither simplicity nor continuity is a virtue in the world of millions of choices. *Dogs might not fit into this switch on/switch off" society.*

2. Changes in social behaviour, caused by new technology such as the Internet.

This new tool, which in a decade or so will be as normal and undramatic as dropping a letter into the mail box, is at the moment the global electronic playground. An uncontrolled assortment of games, products, messages and services has created a new pastime of choice for millions of people. As we have seen, we can even buy 'virtual dogs' for children. The entertainment side of the personal computer and, with that, the fixation Ïon today's version of the Net will decrease with the upcoming introduction of digital TV. However, these two novelties together are likely to cause some changes in the behaviour of hundreds of millions of people. *In my book, we could call this phenomenon the electronic alienation from reality.*

3. Urban concentrations.

The vast majority of the population of the 'first world' lives
in dense communities or large cities. Nature is further and
further away, both physically and, frequently, mentally too.
This development has added to the changes in lifestyles (see
Threat 1) and it has also, no doubt, presented some real challenges for dogs in our present-day society. A parallel development, not least in Europe, is the dislocation of large population groups. New, sometimes incompatible, social habits
can emerge. Breeding fighting dogs and betting on dog
fights is one of the least welcome realities in most countries
in Western Europe today. *Dog ownership faces a lack of open
space and societies are disrupted by destructive uses of dogs.*

4. The easy access to mechanical exercise machines.

Ironically, the body-building and other health-freak crazes
(many of which seem to have their origins in California)
have not only brought with them the focus on a beautiful
body, but hundreds of new mechanical gadgets for physical
exercise. The costs of such equipment decreases from month
to month. The business of marketing exercise machines from
(healthy) mountain bikes to (boring) treadmills is booming.
And because of these new-fangled pursuits, the charm of
natural walks in the forest or old-fashioned jogging circuits,
seems to have been eclipsed. *Sound bodies are more and more
frequently built by sick machines.*

5. The growing influence of special interest groups.

The freedom of expression that even small groups of citizens
enjoy today is, naturally, a healthy sign that the world might
be moving towards real democracy and tangible liberties.
The downside is that the financial success of some special
interest groups has created a new breed of professional 'anti-
something' organisations. It has been said that the final out-
come of the anti-smoking groups formed in the 1980s and
90s, which hopefully will give us a society where no
teenagers smoke, might also have been the heralds of a new
profession. The business of systematic marketing of 'destructive' (as opposed to constructive) policies. Some of the anti-

allergy activists belong to this category, as do the fast-growing 'consumer protection' industries. *The dog world must realise that nothing is sacred to organisations who are out to make a living by being negative.*

6. The lack of mass media content.

The predominant media of today, television and print, offer more and more alternatives, be they TV channels or specialist magazines. Only the latter have, so far, managed to grow naturally, with a deeper and deeper penetration into areas that are important to small but affluent interest groups. The next TV revolution, digital TV, which offers hundreds rather than tens of channels (plus interactivity), will accentuate the problem of lack of content. 'Afternoon' papers, otherwise known as the tabloid press, might soon meet their peers in the electronic world. With the lack of real news and quality content, sensationalist journalism is the first choice for attracting readers. Again, readers and viewers are an absolute necessity to attract advertisers. Without advertising income, sections of the media will die and media plurality shrink to the levels found in Stalin's Soviet Union. *Sadly, dogs have already become a popular target for sensationalism.*

In my home country, Sweden, an unbalanced press debate about docking dogs' tails was the signal for a new media interest in dogs – and not always for the good. The German and British phobia about 'Pitbulls' or 'killer dogs' is a lot more aggressive and even less interested in seeking the facts. *Suddenly, the media do not ask what man does with and to dogs, but what evil things they can allege that dogs have done to man.*

7. The new surrogate-policies of the political world.

Post-World War II, the West saw an unprecedented number of great political minds and also tangible, constructive political ideas put into place. Though the world was in turmoil, determination to act was omnipresent, the money was available (at least in the USA) and forceful leaders made a real impact and solved real problems. Europe was rebuilt, largely thanks to the Marshall Plan. The United Nations managed to reach real and dramatic decisions, such as the birth of the state of Israel. The World Health Organisation battled real killer diseases, such as tuberculosis and malaria, with tangible, hands-on action.

Today, with unemployment looming as a dark cloud over Europe, with unexpected challenges to the very social fabric of the 'Old World', with new forms of media that scare the political establishment because of their global accessibility, fast solutions no longer exist. More and more decisions are made, not to improve the quality of life or society, but to facilitate the selling of 'soundbites' on behalf of a particular politician or political party. Politicians have become marketing men, and their sales success is counted in numbers of votes. The key to votes is media attention. The new political strategy is far too often 'Gallup politics' – decisions tailored to popular (and populist) attitudes resulting in token legislation. Racism (this disgusting problem) is 'fought' by banning words or symbols. Unemployment is lowered and hospital waiting lists shortened by juggling statistics. Sexual discrimination is 'solved' by empty attacks on journalism or advertising. Industrial air pollution is 'tackled' by banning smoking in bars. *The rapidly increasing tendencies to legislate against dogs represent one of the darkest, most cynical examples of surrogate-policies.*

DARK CLOUDS ON THE HORIZON

This is not scaremongering. This is not science fiction. Not even science faction. We don't have to look to stereotypically intolerant societies or totalitarian, inhumane states for evidence of the threat to dogs; many examples of anti-canine legislation exist all over the 'first world'. In Australia, the land of 'Southern Hemisphere cowboys', some cities ban dogs altogether or set quotas for dog ownership per household or building. Several parts of the US are debating indiscriminate bans on certain breeds of dog. Allergy groups pressurise owners of sports or exhibition halls to ban dog shows. France has listed those breeds to be eliminated through complete breeding bans; Scandinavian regional politicians have suggested that dogs should be leashed, even in the fenced-in gardens of dog owners. A Swedish minister demands "the killing of all Pitbulls" (presumably thinking that they are a breed of dog).

In Germany, in some states, certain breeds have to be muzzled by law, and also in Ireland. Also, in some parts of Germany, so-called 'dangerous breeds' pay huge punitive taxes. In Belgium, a draconian anti-dog law was thwarted only because the arrogant minister promoting it was fired. New European countries such as Poland are contemplating legislation against dog ownership, and Spain and Holland also have new canine legislation in the pipeline. Still, this list is just a fraction of the legislation that already exists, or is in the making. For our canine companions, the year 2001 risks becoming a veritable 1984.

THE DOG – MAN'S BEST FRIEND

Society has a duty to look at the new millennium, to look at human/canine bonds and then ask the question, simply and fairly: What are the benefits of dogs and what are the problems? Those involved in the kennel world, in my opinion, bear the main responsibility for repaying our dogs what is their due for more than 20,000 years of loyal companionship.

The benefits of human/canine companionship are, as I have mentioned, more widespread and better known than ever before. But however much they are known to those who benefit from them, they are not, perhaps, properly recognised by society. The obvious canine services include guide dogs for visually handicapped people; police, military and, nowadays perhaps most of all, Customs duties; mine-dog training; dogs used for hunting and environmental control; avalanche dog patrols; tracking dogs used in the search for lost people (especially children); possibly also bomb-detection dogs. It is presumably less well known that dog owners, on average, enjoy a healthier and slightly longer life. Senior citizens offered canine contact stay alert longer and have a better quality of life; handicapped people can use dogs for numerous types of assistance; heart-bypass patients significantly increase their first-year survival rates through dog ownership; and pre-school as well as older children show fewer tendencies to violent behaviour if they have grown up with pets in their immediate vicinity.

In the more technical areas, the mine detection dog is still irreplaceable in clearing landmines (up to 25 per cent more time-efficient than any other electronic or mechanical solution); and recent tragedies such as the bombing of US embassies in Africa highlighted the dramatic difference in rescue work depending on whether it was done with or without the aid of search and rescue dogs. Mildew detection dogs do less dramatic, but financially important work.

In addition to this, we must not forget the regular aspects of family companionship, with and without links to canine sports. For example, a walking in the forest, using the family dog to find edible mushrooms, is both healthy, fun and a money-saving activity. Dog sports are, on the whole, true mass sports. The traditional dog sport, dog showing is, unfortunately, often misinterpreted as a 'beauty contest' for dogs, while the reality is that it is actually an evaluation of soundness and dog-control training. The sport might not seem to be all that exciting to the public at large, but it ensures the general long-term health of dogs, the sound breeding of pedigree dogs (which are part of man's cultural heritage) and also promotes the safe handling of dogs.

While we have every justification to deplore sensationalist journalism that undermines canine rights, we also have an equal responsibility to analyse possible problems with dog ownership in today's social environment. One of the best ways forward in any country is to obtain and carefully study official statistics gathered by the authorities. How many police reports against dogs/dog owners have there been? What are the cases about? Which breeds were involved (so which then need to be analysed further)? Are there any common denominators among the dog owners? What punishments have been imposed by the authorities? And how has the dog world responded, if a country or area has experienced real problems?

One of the best sources for a brief sample analysis is the German study *The Dog in Cities* (Der Stadthund). It shows that, during a five-year period in Germany, 21,126 incidents involving dogs were reported. This, for the statisticians, means 89 incidents reported per city, i.e. fewer than 8 per city per year. In a total of 208 cities, 8,356 reports claimed bodily harm, of which 76 per cent were classified as 'light', 20 per cent as 'medium' and 4 per cent as 'serious'. As for the penalties imposed, 6,000 were expressed as 'verbal warnings'. and 5,144 as mandatory leashing of the dog. In 282 cases the dogs were put to sleep, i.e. about 56 cases a year. Whether this ultimate penalty was given to a high or low number is a matter for debate. To animal lovers, every single one that could have been avoided represents a failure of the kennel world – and of society. (Interestingly, comparing the breeds listed as 'dangerous' in some German states, there is little correlation between the listing and the actual number of reported incidents, as there are popular breeds on the list of 'dangerous dogs' with fewer than 10 reports against them in the entire five-year period. This gives us reason to suspect that the 'dangerous dogs' lists are either unrelated to any knowledge of canine or breed-specific behaviour, or that they are severely politically influenced).

Another picture is painted when we realise that there were, in 1998 and 1999 alone, some incidents in Europe where human beings were killed in incidents involving dogs. In almost all of these cases there were other aspects to the case than sheer aggressiveness on the part of the animal. However, every single severe incident, not to mention lethal accident, is a reason to look for underlying causes, as well as for possible action to be taken in response. This is one of the main reasons why this debate must be taken forward!

MAN – DOG'S BEST FRIEND?

In every crisis there is always an opportunity (the Chinese language even has the same symbol for the words 'crisis' and 'opportunity'). Glancing back at the seven main threats against dogs, we can list at least eight reasons why the human/canine bond could and should survive. Here are my predictions of trends and developments that, hopefully, will create opportunities.

1. Human adaptability to threat and change.

Clusters of humans, which we call society, have always formed, in order to achieve protection, hunting efficiency and, later, teamwork, which further increases working efficiency and affluence of the members. Excesses are also countered by trends in opposing directions. Already today, we see an increased interest in Nature. Mainstream TV successfully screens programmes about wildlife, natural wonders and animals. Interest in the small, the home-grown and in personal roots is as great as ever. As for musical tastes, folk music and even regional music is back in fashion (nowadays not even every Eurovision Song Contest composition sounds like standard pop music. Thank you Ireland!). From a wider perspective, societies and institutions are waking up to the necessity of creating a new, more sustainable world. This includes sustainable production and sustainable consumption. Pollution and decreasing natural resources will force us humans to change our way of living. In the end, it will mean genuine respect for Nature and the environment. *The dog has a place in a new, sustainable attitude to life.*

2. Human isolation.

Never in human history have so many people lived so near to each other and still been so lonely. This is why, as an exanple, Internet-based home shopping will capture only part of our daily shopping routines i.e. the type of shopping that is a boring necessity (I call it the 'toilet-paper shopping syndrome').The counter-trend will be that shopping malls evolve into entertainment centres, where people meet, chat and enjoy social life. People do not, on the whole, love to hang around in fast-food restaurants, but millions enjoy the company to be found in a British pub, a Brazilian coffeehouse, a French bistro or a Belgian or Dutch cafe. *Tomorrow's citizens will battle against loneliness: consequently, companionship with dogs will retain its attractiveness.*

3. The boom in mass media.

The mass media development that has created sensationalist journalism also offers an opportunty. To take one example, hundreds of digital TV channels, without proper and interesting content, will offer a golden opportunity for new and interesting canine sports to capture public interest. *Remember, some 70-80 per cent of Western TV viewers are basically positive towards dogs.*

4. Increasing leisure time and the quest for new activities.

Another example of the reverse side of the coin. If the kennel world can recreate itself, view the past and the present with critical yet creative eyes, and develop new sports – or shall we call them products? – then there is a receptive market waiting. A market that is always willing to try something new at least once, and something exciting several more times. *The success of some new canine sports, such as Agility, Lure Coursing, Flyball etc., show that dog sports have ample scope for new ideas.*

5. The search for new, healthy lifestyles.

It has been said that, in the new California-type lifestyle, the body is the modern temple. Through activities that border on religious rites, people seek, if not eternal, then at least ever-longer lives. At the same time, health services are becoming increasingly costly for 'first world' governments (in some countries with backward social systems, such as even the US, the mere thought of a European-style social conscience is a mathematical horror story). Preventative and (soon) pre-emptive health care is a political must. *Few hobbies are better suited to fill this void of health-promotion than both existing and new forms of canine companionship.*

6. The fundamental social problems of the West.

The youth crime figures; the impersonalised care of the elderly; the mechanised treatment of the sick; the social neo-cynicism; all these things lead societies to look for an alternative way. Nature is sometimes wonderful in her uncompromising realism. In the field of medicine, big, super-scientific companies are scouring the Amazonian jungle for new clues to old illnesses (and breakthrough cures for new ones). Our social structure will do the same. *Mental burn-out will one day be countered by a widespread realisation of the need to re-open the dialogue with Nature.*

7. The fear of breaking away from Nature and Man's past.

It is hardly a coincidence that, even in our modern world, we can access masses of material written by people specialising in theology and animal rights. Religion and spirituality spring, not from something man-made, but from human insufficiency in the face of Nature, time and the universe. In daily life, the last tangible link between man and Nature is his closest live companion, the dog If we cut the last cord linking us to out origins, the consequences will be devastating. *Man will realise this in time: human/canine links are older than man-made 'civilisation'.*

8. The unique qualities of the canine species.
We have far from exhausted all the talents of the canine species.

CAMPAIGNS – THE LAST RESORT OF THE KENNEL WORLD?
Since 1996, I have had the privilege of being part of a Swedish Kennel Club team dealing with a pro-canine development project. This might be the single most versatile, pre-emptive distribution of information by any canine association in the world. Hence, I have been asked to look at the dog world of today and tomorrow from the perspective of a professional communicator. In the past, I also had an opportunity to work with the WWF (World Wide Fund for Nature) for a number of years. This period taught me that things *are* possible and results *can* be achieved. The number-one enemy of the dog world, not least the international one, is a lack of self-esteem and an absence of radical thought. The WWF can, in this respect, act as a valuable example for dog lovers.

It is not my aim here to list all the opportunities, as well as the options, as they exist. Partly because that is the idea behind the entire book. Partly because it takes more than one person, and a great deal of new thinking, to come up with a comprehensive list of ideas and recommendations. But this is where we started in 1996:

The simple truth
One cannot preserve without developing. To stand still

means moving backwards. To keep quiet means communicating the negatives. The kennel world must decide, and fast, whether it wants to move ahead or start sliding into obscurity.

The next consequence is that canine organisations have to decide whether they want to be active or reactive. Creating a lasting future for our canine companions must be an ongoing, proactive process.

The unpalatable truth

A 'campaign' is never a solution. A campaign is a tool. Even the best intentions and the most brilliant creative solutions do not take a campaign beyond temporary relief of the current issue. In the kennel world, short-term campaign thinking can certainly salve our consciences a little. But it will provide little in the way of solutions for the new century, let alone the new millennium. This does not mean we should not advocate action when a crisis occurs. For instance, those dog lovers, breed clubs and canine organisations that have got together and taken action against sudden anti-canine legislation deserve nothing but praise. In such cases, you have a crisis, a clear objective, a timeframe for solving the problem and a result. Hopefully a positive one!

The dog world must rethink and start planning from the basics. I am now talking about something global in scope, which must be ready within four or five years from now. Otherwise, time will have run out. I'm not talking about new committees, new task forces or even a new structure of national kennel clubs. I am talking about a fundamental change of attitudes, ambitions and resources, to promote and secure the rights of canines in society.

Over time, the sheer versatility of the dog is the best guarantee of survival. The functions and roles of the dog must be supported, enhanced and communicated. If the political world makes anti-canine moves because of lack of knowledge and understanding, it is still the fault of the kennel world.

What we do not know we cannot use. Positive functions in which the potential of dogs can be increased must be identified and placed in full focus. More and more cities and countries must use dogs to help decrease youth violence, improve care of the elderly and offer services to the well-known sectors, such as the police and the military. The kennel world must also make an all-out effort to build upon the enormous mass media potential of new canine sports.

The 20th century saw many great speakers and communicators. One of the lesser known is Barry Day (at least, outside the advertising world, though many of us have seen and admired his campaign called *Your Right To Choose*). He wrote, some 20 years ago, a book called *What We Have Here Is A Failure To Communicate*. This is exactly the problem of the kennel world globally. The canine bodies, or kennel clubs, in each active market and also from a cross-border perspective, need a communications strategy, with a ten-year target. They also need professionals and resources. Resources do not always equal money, but they do always mean:

1. Trained staff, and
2. Continuity, continuity, continuity!

Back in 1996 I took a shot at both the existing advertising of the Swedish Kennel Club, as well as the (lack of) involvement of a number of dog food and equipment manufacturers. What the dog world needs (and our dogs deserve) is to be taken seriously. In the past, the Swedish Kennel Club had run a humorous, attention-grabbing poster campaign around the age-old theme 'The Dog – Man's best Friend', without offering a single example of this already well-known claim. The response could only be one of uninterested agreement. It is also called 'kicking in open doors'. The new strategy must be to prove the proposition that our society needs its dogs, to demonstrate it and to repeat it over and over again with the use of varying, effective examples.

Any effective communication starts from attention. This is not really a problem. There are many new, many unknown and also many (both well known and less familiar) visually dramatic examples of the benefits of dogs.

For communication to work, it must be credible. As the old advertising experts used to say 'give them a reason to believe'. Again, we have ample available proof of the claims. Also, one decision that must be made, ideally internationally, is to form a new body whereby the national (and regional) kennel organisations have access to new, interesting examples of dogs in the service of our societies. This must be an ongoing task, which also assumes organised internal communication among the various national kennel club bodies. This must also be an area where dog food and equipment manufacturers can play a key role in support of the kennel organisations.

PRODUCT DEVELOPMENT – THE KEY TO LASTING SUCCESS

The existing, but still relatively new, initiatives in canine sports must be developed, researched (understanding the extent and depth of interest among regular consumers) and presented to the media. The new mass media, such as digital TV, as noted under 'risks' and 'opportunities', will have to work hard to fill the gap in programme content. But contenders to fill the gap cannot afford to be inactive. Hence the kennel world must begin the process urgently, first developing the sports it already has.

The step towards a totally new package of canine sports seems to be a large one, but nevertheless fascinating. There is no doubt that we should refine and test existing novelties (e.g. Agility etc.) in parallel with a search for even more radical, creative ideas.

The canine sports of tomorrow must be developed by looking both through the viewfinder of the TV camera and the magnifying glass of the cynological expert.

There is also a need to work more closely with commercial stakeholders. For far too long, the leading dog food companies have been seen as generous donors of some money, plus colourful displays at dog shows. Sponsorship today does not mean handing out money like a friendly, benevolent grandfather. It means a strategy of co-operation. Using the skills of leading marketing companies, the kennel world must urgently access TV, at least on a trial basis. Now, I am not talking about essential and morally wonderful programmes, such as France's *30 Million Amies*, which take on a social role in presenting animals and also appealing for new homes for homeless pets.

We must start discussing how dog-related sports can be exploited in real-life situations. We must calculate canine potential for the advertising sales market. Feel free to call me 'commercial'. Commerce and trade, including advertising, is a lifeline for any functioning society (though I have to admit that I suffered, even though I am a former sportsman, when I saw the over-commercialisation of the Atlanta Olympics). We must test the repeat interest of the viewers of these programmes; research the viewer profile; find the optimal length of dog sports events; and work hand in hand with the media (including support media, such as newspapers) to develop experience in creating general interest in the sport. When this know-how has been obtained, it is likely that the kennel world will either need to attract its own media experts, to deal with TV and other media outlets, or it will need to sign long-term contracts with leading pet food manufacturers. As to how to start creating totally new canine sports, I suggest we need to involve as many young pro-dog activists as possible. Each creative group or task force should then have a few members with media backgrounds.

Another element of the 'canine product' is the creation of closer links with the academic world. When, as an example, Dr Ingemar Norling in Sweden first presented his study on the effect of dogs within paediatric care, it became both a media event and a government lobbying tool. The day when the kennel world can prove, with hard facts and sometimes precise numbers, the benefits derived from liaison with canines, then and only then can we talk about government lobbying on an ongoing scale. Political contacts always start from fact-based representations. In addition, these facts must serve a dual purpose – they must help the politicians do their job and they must be relevant to the cause of fact-presenters.

PRIORITIES FOR THE FUTURE

The need for a global kennel organisation is a theme to which we must revert. Frequently! Today's FCI is presumably a lot better at doing what it is asked to do than the average dog owner realises. It also has potential to expand within Europe, as well as in South America. But such expansion is a task that can be left for a while. The need to establish canine rights in the developed world must be given top priority. The big question is: Is the FCI being asked to do the right work? The unequivocal answer is: No! Again, the blame is not with the FCI but with its members. The international organisation of the future must have a mandate to represent canine interests to top-level organisations, such as the European Union and even the United Nations. Here is a list of other requirements:

1. It must have international-class communications capabilities.
2. It must be the driving force in 'product development'.
3. It must accept the co-ordinating function for incoming information about academic projects, relevant results and other data that are essential in national political work.
4. It must have economic and strategic business competence to work closely with the dog-related industries.
5. It must set its targets high.

There is no reason why dog sports enthusiasts could not, within the next 30 years, create a global 'family community' resembling that of a miniature Olympic movement.

It is not pessimistic, but realistic, to state that the kennel world cannot survive unless it takes responsibility for the coming generations. Schools are our best friends of the future. Securing impartial information, and also imparting information on how to live in a multi-species society, must start with schoolbooks and education. This is another full-time task for a kennel organisation in the future.

Finally, a moral issue. As we, hopefully, embark on a path of new thinking in order to secure the role of dogs in the third millennium, we do not have the right to neglect the wild cousins of modern dogs. Unless we also work to safe-guard the survival of the wild canine species, we have little or no right to dream about a better future for dog sports! The environment is the responsibility of each and every citizen. To remember the canines that live free in Nature must be a matter of honour for every dog owner.

Chapter Four
URBANISATION AND ITS CONSEQUENCES

Within the last 50 years, the development of human society – and the impact on living creatures that share our lives – has been shocking. Urbanisation has intensified, and ever-growing numbers of people crowd into an ever-shrinking living area. German bureaucrats, and others in neighbouring countries, have severely restricted 'land allotment' in desirable suburban areas, in order to stem the tide of requests for building permits. People and their pets are being forced to live in an ever-smaller area.

MEMORIES OF THE PAST
I remember back in 1944, when I was a young boy, I found my first dog under the Christmas tree. My father had granted this, my dearest wish, despite the earlier bombardment of the city of Pforzheim. This event influenced the rest of my life.

For a thirteen-year-old, my little dog 'Strolch' was a unique experience. Everything that Professor Bengler has written about the significance of dogs for children and adolescents proved true in my case. The little guy soon became the centre of my life; however, the story had an unhappy ending. Strolch was confiscated shortly after French troops moved in, and spent the rest of his life elsewhere as the companion of a dark-haired beauty.

As a result, a German Shepherd trotted into my life. During this period of great collective hunger, a strong, protective dog was the dearest wish of a large section of the population. These were times in which our dogs took on the function of true defenders of their human families. Anyone who experienced the years directly after the War knows what I am talking about.

Before the 1945 bombardment, Pforzheim had a population of about 80,00. I remember how much space we kids and our dogs had, and we could use it undisturbed. During these years, unleashed dogs were constantly encountered in every part of the city. You see, I knew pretty well when, and where, I could meet my special 'dog friends'. There were meadows and fields all around the city. No one thought that canines might have to be kept on a leash. Basically, the dogs all got along with one another, even when there was an occasional disagreement concerning the hierarchy within the group. We laid trails through gardens and out across the fields for our dogs, and no one had the slightest objection. It was absolutely normal for a family to own a dog. Even when a large, unleashed dog approached, no one crossed to the other side of the road.

At the same time, my wife grew up in the 'Zoo-Viertel' located in the middle of Düsseldorf. She remembers a childhood in which, if you didn't own a dog yourself, you could always collect the neighbour's dog to go for a walk, or to play 'horsey' around the paddock. No one forbade children their games. Long walks in a canine-friendly atmosphere, even in the centre of Düsseldorf, were quite usual. No one got upset about the fact that the dogs had to relieve themselves occasionally. Street cleaners were responsible for cleanliness on a daily basis. The children's playground was free of broken glass, empty cans and used condoms. The existence of dog defecation was recognised as something completely natural – a tiny threat to the environment when compared to the volume of man-made pollution now produced every day.

I can still remember, quite a few years ago, an informative discussion on *Club 2*, a Viennese television programme. Six canine experts gathered for the occasion to discuss how much living space is left for our dogs. The main discussion centred on the question, 'Are dogs a dangerous threat to humans?'. I look back on this three-and-a-half-hour open-ended discussion with pleasure because, at the time, one could still rationally discuss (not just argue about) the topic of conversation. What particularly sticks in my mind about the Viennese standpoint was that the panel of experts attempted to deal with the subject seriously, exploring how, from an animal protection perspective, one could even try to own and maintain a canine in any major city in the world. They talked about the fact that (due to the height of canine noses) urban dogs were constantly exposed to car exhaust fumes, and about which health problems would occur as a result.

Even then, though, urban dogs were referred to from the 'danger' standpoint; for example, statistical data was produced to emphasise how much canine faeces the city had to remove from the streets per year. Before the discussion, I had diligently researched the topic of conversation and could reassure TV viewers that the possibility of being bitten in Vienna by a dangerous dog was about as likely as being struck by lightning.

At the conclusion of our discussion, we all unanimously agreed that, in spite of all the difficulties involved in keeping a dog in the city, for many people the dog is the last vital 'bridge to Nature' in an urban environment. Our four-legged friends make life in a concrete jungle easier to bear. One only has to observe the example of the English Garden in Munich with its kaleidoscopic display of dogs and their owners. It highlights the great human desire for a close partnership with canines. While in New York, I had the opportunity of visiting one of the city's small, designated, extremely well-frequented dog playgrounds. There are so many lonely people living in urban areas whose only companion is a dog. Think of senior citizens who would otherwise feel completely useless without a pet!

REALITIES OF THE PRESENT

By the introduction of specific, drastic measures, some larger cities are currently trying to make it impossible to keep a dog. Comprehensive leash laws in all parks, the closure of formerly fenced open areas where dogs could run free, and exaggeratedly imposed canine taxes make it more and more difficult to own a pet. Dog owners have already begun to reconsider the possibility of being able to reasonably maintain a dog in the city. As a nose-orientated animal living in a concrete desert, a dog can hardly enjoy the experience of following a scent any more.

Under these circumstances, with all park areas banned for animals and an unnaturally restricted life on the leash, dog owners must possess an extremely strong love of animals, and a great deal of self-sacrifice, to accompany their pets on a daily walk. They must deal, in addition, with the fact that a canine has certain basic needs. Nowadays, it is a matter of fact that every responsible dog owner uses a plastic bag or 'poop scoop'. Certainly, this isn't an ideal answer to the problem, but it shows the willingness of dog owners to comply with public opinion. An alternative solution could be taking trips with your four-legged friend to the surrounding countryside, so that he can freely stretch his legs. One can only hope that such countryside is available within a reasonable distance of an urban area. In any case, I immensely admire dog owners who surmount such difficulties; this is additional proof of how much people need dogs, and how much dogs mean to them.

A CHANGE IN RURAL ATTITUDES

It would be a mistake merely to single out life in the big city. Things don't look that much better in smaller communities either. One thing remains incomprehensible to me. Only 50 years ago, it was seen as absolutely natural that roosters crow, dogs bark, and cats roam free. In my Swabian homeland, horse and cattle carts were not uncommon, and, when nature called, these large animals would deposit 'fertilizer', which would be gathered enthusiastically by hobby gardeners.

Today, even the rural population is already so alienated from animals that an unleashed dog is tolerated only up to a certain point. Fear of dogs, unfounded as it may seem in rural areas, is widespread, even though these people should be accustomed to animals, having lived with them since childhood.

Let me recount a personal experience. A neighbour, a teacher and a dedicated father insisted that his six-year-old boy should always kick an approaching dog. Luckily, the lad's schoolmates finally convinced him that no living thing would allow itself to be kicked without defending itself.

Today, rural canines very seldom find much tolerance in their environment; the anti-dog lobby is already well established in the countryside. It is absolutely astounding how far the rural population has removed itself from the 'Yes-to-Nature' standpoint.

Therefore, it is not only urbanisation and the lack of space that makes life with our dogs difficult. People's natural, unselfconscious behaviour towards dogs has fundamentally changed. This subject will be discussed in depth in the next chapter.

Chapter Five
MISUNDERSTANDINGS ABOUT DOGS

There is hardly anything more fascinating than an in-depth study of the domestication of the canine and the destiny awaiting him in his relationship with Mankind.

A SEE-SAW RELATIONSHIP

Throughout history, there have been, and still are, many ups and downs for the dog, ranging from the Egyptian god Anubis to a stray mutt, from a kicked companion to a prized hunting dog, and to the watchdog tied up pitifully on a chain. The oldest household pet has not always found a respectful and appreciative lifelong partner in man.

Loud praises are sung to the well-behaved canine. Our dogs accompanied us and sacrificed themselves for us during two horrible world wars. There very many untold stories of how dogs have risked their lives serving their masters in every country in the civilised world. Just think of the hundreds of people saved by the tremendous performance of earthquake and avalanche rescue dogs.

As humans, we should not overlook the needs of our dogs, as socially-orientated, communal animals requiring the closest kind of 'pack' man/dog relationship. Yet we commit the worst sort of cruelty to canines by confining them in kennels, or isolating them out of doors. An isolated dog soon becomes desperately unhappy – or dangerous! But the blame for such negative development lies more with their two-legged caretakers and masters than with the dogs themselves.

The domestic canine has lived by our side for 15,000 years, and standing opposite him is ignorant Man!

REASONS FOR IGNORANCE

The majority of uninformed people have received their

knowledge – or lack of it – almost literally direct from their mother's milk, passed down from ignorant parents, grandparents and other relatives. The most important alternative is 'hearsay' information from neighbours and friends, usually exchanged in the atmosphere of a comfortable get-together accompanied by alcohol! Every civilised person knows that one doesn't buy and operate a new washing machine, kitchen appliance or car without having read the instructions. But dogs? Of course, everyone already knows about that subject! You don't have to learn – all you need are the proverbial green fingers! The truth is that rearing a dog correctly is a great deal more difficult than growing a cabbage!

People's ignorance of the basic needs of their canines is frightening! Humans know how to operate complicated computers, are familiar with the world of technology and can fly through outer space. But only very few realise that our domestic dogs, as living creatures, are far more complicated and varied in their behaviour than any technology. If Man wants to fully enjoy his canine companion, he must adapt himself to the natural needs of his pet, must care for him according to his breed, and must maintain him, train him and feed him.

Did you ever learn in school what wonderful creatures dogs are, or can be? Have you seen any television programme that has transmitted real knowledge about the domestic dog? Or have you found a current educational programme offering courses that could correct your lack of knowledge on the subject?

EDUCATING CHILDREN

Let me be more direct. How is the image of the dog transmitted to the toddler, then from the child to the adolescent? Mother threatens the young child: 'If you don't behave, then a dog will bite you!' In our old fairytales, we consistently encounter the distorted image of the dangerous wolf. He eats grandmother, Little Red Riding Hood, the three little pigs and is a threat to all household pets! Our own distorted man-made image is far removed from the factual knowledge amassed about the wolf by modern behavioural scientists. As a result, latent fears rise to the surface in every child when he meets a dog, and overwhelm the natural childish desire to hug such a sweet, cuddly, friendly, tail-wagging creature!

As with many things in life, the rule here is: 'What little Johnny doesn't learn, big John never learns'. All the former misunderstandings can be sorted out, but only if the effort starts with the right home upbringing. Parents who suffer from canine phobias will very seldom have children who interact with dogs freely and in an unprejudiced way. Parental fears are transmitted to their children during the early behaviour development phase of the latter.

At this point, kindergartens and schools should step in and take responsibility in an attempt to correct the problem. Of course, in larger cities there are 'zoo schools', that introduce exotic animals and teach children about them. Unfortunately, no dogs are normally presented to visiting classes, an initiative which would help reduce the fears children bring with them from home. Then there are the 'petting zoos', excellent establishments that our children love to visit. But, even in a petting zoo, there is no opportunity for a child to build a relationship with a domestic dog.

The dog, today, is prevented from being a social companion by parents, kindergartens, schools, vicious press stories and persistent, irrational, subconscious fears. Such factors have created the enormous anti-dog lobby that has now arisen. These 'child protectors' are, in part, responsible for causing certain situations, in which some children are actually bitten by dogs. The usual cause is not the 'aggressive dog', but the disturbed child, who takes one look at a peaceful, friendly dog and runs away screaming loudly! Have you ever observed how unkind poorly-raised children can be to a dog: beating against the garden fence, throwing rocks, yelling, whooping and provoking him from a safe distance? Parents and teachers are the guilty ones. They are responsible, not the children, for misrepresenting the reality of dogs in the minds of many people. The real cause of many accidents involving dogs is fear itself.

If only our children had learned to live with dogs, the number of bitten children would plummet by about 90 per cent, because all scientific research points to the fact that, in only about 10 per cent of actual cases involving dogs, is the dog the cause of the accident. In all other cases, the cause is the human behaviour.

Our children are not guilty, only a society that obviously doesn't deem it necessary to provide its children with correct knowledge about the dog. Later in this book, I will provide scientific reasearch to prove how desperately children need dogs. It's about time we began to clear up current misunderstandings, and the resulting alienation of our dogs, by providing comprehensive and accurate information on the subject.

Chapter Six
VICTIMS OF A MEDIA CAMPAIGN

There is a fundamental law in journalism: Good news equals no news; bad news equals increased sales!

Every day, across the world, planes are in the air. How about the headline: 'Aeroplanes land safe and sound'? No journalist is interested in the success story of air travel. Why would anyone want to report something as boringly safe as air travel? But readers can be certain to find stories on the few air catastrophes each year when Man, or technology, or both, failed!

It's a similar situation with our dogs. Who is interested in the fact that 98 per cent of our four-legged friends live a completely normal life in public? However, if at some time an incident occurs involving a canine, a hailstorm of negative headlines appears, to the detriment of all dog owners.

LACK OF OBJECTIVITY
In order to throw some light on the subject, the 'Deutsche Städtetages' (the German National Council of Cities) recently published the results of a long-term study spanning 10 years. They came to the conclusion, after comparing two five-year periods, that incidents with dogs had been reduced by half. When you look through the media, where is the reporting of such a discovery? Objective statistics such as these are omitted wholesale and, thus, sensational reports make much more impact on the public consciousness.

Who doesn't remember the 'Man without a Face', who was paraded on a number of German television broadcasts? This 'victim' was dragged from one TV station to another, where he bemoaned his fate and what 'Kampfhunde' (fighting dogs) did to him. But when was it mentioned on any one of these programmes that he, and he alone, was personally responsible for his misfortune?

We know now, after the event, how horribly he tortured his dogs and that, when he tripped in their kennel, he suffered the consequences. It could be seen as a just punishment. What's more, I would like to emphasise that it would have been far more responsible on the part of the authorities to confiscate this sadist's animals before the accident took place. The fact that this background information was not released, in order to heighten the sensational newsworthiness of the story, violates journalistic ethics. Evidently, such ethics are, from time to time, traded off in favour of financial profits and higher ratings.

THE CASE FOR PERSONAL RESPONSIBILITY

Please note at this point, that in any contact with animals, even housepets, there is a certain 'tierische Restgefahr' or residual risk. But every individual is responsible for him or herself, and I have been told that the annual quota of accidents involving horses is higher and more serious than that involving dogs. This statistic isn't intended to cover anything up – every incident in which persons are injured causes great human suffering and is extremely regrettable – but human life can be threatened in a variety of ways. Just think of daily traffic! But I believe that, for the media, the dog seems an especially attractive target and that negative coverage raises TV ratings and sells newspapers.

Also, the problem is not confined to the media campaign against dogs or to cases involving 'biting dogs'. Statistics from the 'Deutsche Städtetages' (the German National Council of Cities), reveal that the highest number of 'offensive' incidents are noise disturbance caused by barking dogs and dog faeces. Now, I'd like to tell you a story on the subject of dog excrement. One evening, after a drinking contest, some journalists decided to make a bet. The object of the bet was a fictitious magazine named *Kot and Koter (Faeces and Fifi)*. This extremely interesting magazine was never published, but for five years its bogus editor-in-chief was interviewed on one talkshow after another. He performed his role well and answered (in a 'beer-honest' voice) all questions put to him about how his successful new magazine was in tremendous demand on the German market. His betting buddies had a great time playing this trick on their colleagues. But the public relations damage inflicted on dogs and their owners, as a result of their 'fun', obviously mattered rather less to these jokers.

THE WAY FORWARD

To sum up, the topic of dog ownership in 2001 raises a number of critical questions. It is the responsibility of dedicated journalists and dog owners to find meaningful answers to these questions. The solution to the problems I have outlined lies not in denying them but in starting to take them seriously. We must discuss them out loud: that is the goal of this book. Objectivity and personal responsibility are required in any basic analysis of what chance our dogs have to continue as Man's companion, throughout this millennium.

Chapter Seven

DOGS AND POLITICIANS

Politicians and the media are closely linked with each other. When hysteria is whipped up against fighting dogs by the media, politicians are only too happy to profit from this popular theme. Under the cover of actually doing something for their voters, they seize the opportunity to demagogically increase their own popularity.

ABSURDITY IN THE UK

A series of political excesses was initiated in, of all places, the UK, the most canine-friendly country in Europe. Let me quote myself commenting on this outbreak of hysteria: "It seems as though the same law exists for every democracy on earth: if a political party loses ground in the last election, officials jump on the bandwagon of 'fighting dogs', thus trying to take advantage of the psychotic fear generated by the media, in order to win back votes. In this way, a similar campaign was fuelled by an unfortunate accident with a six-year-old and a Pitbull".

Even the British press marvelled at the 'witchhunt' led by then Home Secretary Kenneth Baker and supported by the Prime Minister Margaret Thatcher.

British politicians had the American Pitbull in their sights, of which dogs there were 10,000 living in Britain. The absurdity of this law was that not only were Pitbulls targeted for the list of banned canines, but also mongrels which were the results of random cross-breeding. This law opened the door for years of litigation, while the confiscated pets were deported and held in an animal shelter at the owners' expense. Most ridiculous of all, the State was not required to prove any allegation; rather, the individual dog owner had to prove that his pet was not a Pitbull mix!

A leading article in the newspaper *The Independent* mirrors the level and tone of the British debate. The newspaper called for an expansion of the law to include the Rottweiler, "that the Nazis used in concentration camps". Furthermore, in the same paper, the Dobermann was identified as "the favourite dog of the communist police in Eastern Europe during the Cold War". There are, after all, around 100,000 Rottweilers and a few thousand Dobermanns in England. Why should the law still allow them to run around freely and unmolested?

This sort of demagogic discrimination is simply unacceptable for reasonable people, but, among the general public, it finds much resonance and acceptance. Yet it must be stressed that all currently available scientific information is unanimous in concluding that the level of risk attached to dogs cannot be quantified according to the specific breed. The genetic factor is very low in comparison to environmental influences, which are, of course, controlled by humans. The real reasons for aggressive canine behaviour are mainly the socialisation and training received from people, or, more accurately, the lack of socialisation and incorrect training!

FEARS FUELLED IN AMERICA

Britain is not the first country to have supported similarly prejudiced legal initiatives. The USA became the initial front-runner by sanctioning drastic laws in a number of states. Allow me to quote Vicki Hearne, a courageous American animal defender, who said in her book *Bandit*: "But look: in 1987, according to the estimate of the Endangered Breed Association, 35,000 people took their bull-breed dogs to pounds and humane societies to be killed, most of them Pitbulls or something someone thought was a Pitbull. There was television and newspaper coverage of people queueing up with their dogs to have them killed. They did this because they had read in the newspaper that their dogs were dangerous, liable to 'turn on them' at any moment, or because their spouses and neighbours had read that, or because..."

Can you imagine a more terrible vision than the sight of

35,000 people taking their pets to humane societies to be killed? The basis for this mass hysteria was laws from the 1970s and 80s in certain American states which triggered a canine programme that anyone experimenting with anti-canine laws should always bear in mind.

THE SITUATION IN GERMANY

The Anglo-Saxon principle of 'law and order' seems to be unusually inspiring for German politicians. Instead of studying the legislative repercussions of such laws, they crank up their own legislative machine. After the federal government sensibly refused to take the initiative, individual states introduced their own legislation. Out of a total of sixteen states, only four remain without any legal restrictions – and these four are busily putting together their own legislative package.

The first laws were imposed (how could it be otherwise?) by the state of Bavaria. This state holds the record for having the highest penalty fees, extending up to DM 100,000.

Following Bavaria's lead, the cities and states of Bremen, Hamburg, Hessen, Rheinland-Pfalz, Saarland and Sachsen each set penalty fees extending up to DM 10,000. Before moving to another state, every German citizen must check with the authorities as to whether his dog is allowed or is subject to any restrictions.

PROFIT FROM PREJUDICE

Local politicians have also discovered how they can profit financially, thanks to general canine hysteria. I had the opportunity of talking to the mayor of the first community to impose a 'fighting dog' tax, in the television broadcast described earlier. He emphasised that his goal, by imposing this tax, was to rid his community of bull breeds. Upon enquiring as to how many fighting dogs lived in his community, I received the astounding answer, "None". It appeared that, in his community a few years previously, there lived one dog owner whose dog was involved in an incident, and, as a result, a new tax was introduced as a precaution for the future.

'Fighting dog' taxes have been raised, in some cases, to ten times the amount one would normally pay for a 'normal' dog. The action comes close to imposing an illegal 'Erdrosselungssteuer' ('strangle' tax). We have 'fighting dog' taxes costing up to DM 1800 per year. Just to give you an idea of how financially important dog taxes are for city treasuries: in 1998, the city of Berlin profited by collecting DM 23,000,000 in canine taxes, DM 240 for the first dog owned, and for every additional dog DM 360. And this amount hasn't yet been modified to include a 'fighting dog' tax, which is currently under discussion. In any case, for city officials, the suspected 'dangerousness' of dogs has brought with it a welcome monetary supplement. Meanwhile, more and more German dog owners are forced to take their pets to animal shelters, because they feel overwhelmed by the imposed restrictions. I will have more to say later about what suffering this causes, particularly for children, in some families.

A LEGISLATIVE BANDWAGON

Berlin has recently captured public attention with plans for new legislation. The 'Rasseliste' (a list of selected canine breeds) was, again typically, a topic of interest in the election. The Rottweiler and the Dobermann were two of the breeds on the list. Planned legislation would require the owners of dogs on the list to have an ownership licence that is preceded by a personal background investigation. This licence and accompanying background check would have to be renewed every two years. Dog ownership would be restricted in apartment buildings. A general leash and muzzle requirement would be imposed and a mandatory document witnessed by a public official – at the dog owner's expense – would attest to the dog's friendliness towards people and other animals. The SPD party unmistakably declared that their goal was to eliminate all large dogs from the city. In addition, a member of the 'Grünen' (Green Party) specified, "I can only imagine dogs being kept behind high chain-link fences".

DOG LOVERS FIGHT BACK

However, the 1999 Berlin election demonstrated that this

type of fishing for popular support doesn't always bring in the desired number of votes. The anti-dog political parties suffered a considerable defeat, while dog-friendly parties won the support of Berlin's citizens. Before the election, dog-friendly politicians had openly declared that they did not plan to change any laws or regulations concerning dog ownership.

So, something positive at last! Before the Berlin election, two animal protection groups organised a demonstration of support for the dog with the title: "Wake up! Vote!". The demonstration package included distribution of 20,000 leaflets and the appearance of hundreds of posters. Local businesses also supported the drive. Wouldn't it be wonderful if dog lovers everywhere, encompassing supporters of all breeds, could come together to form a unified front against misguided politicians?

The state of Schleswig-Holstein has obviously not taken heed of the example set by Berlin. The minister of the interior called for "a general law against bull breeds" and specified requirements for castration, plus an examination proving good temperament and a muzzle requirement. He said, "the public wants action taken". One can only hope that the citizens of Schleswig-Hostein follow Berlin's lead by voting out the parties in question.

EXPERT OPINION

The German 'Tierschützbund e.V.' (Animal Protection Agency) released the following statement in a press report: "The Tierschützbund appeals to the public not to contribute to the general hysteria directed towards 'fighting dogs'. There is no specific 'fighting dog' breed. Public demands won't find a solution to the problem. They only feed the hysteria and make it worse... Stop random discrimination against responsible dog owners and their pets... Inherited breed-related aggressiveness has been occasionally documented only in certain individual bloodlines, and cannot be generally expanded to include entire canine breeds. In the majority of cases, the owner or caretaker is responsible for accidents involving aggression with dogs."

The 'Verband für das Deutsche Hundewesen e.V.' (the

Canine Club of Germany) presented four documented scientific reports dealing with this absurd discussion. The
canine experts, Dr Helga Eichelberg (Bonn), Dr Dorit
Feddersen-Petersen (Kiel), Professor Dr J Unselen (Munich)
and Professor Dr Wolfram Hamman unanimously found
that there is no scientific factual basis warranting discrimination against particular canine breeds. The University of
Vienna drew up an analogous report for the state of
Steiermark that forced the region to annul existing prejudi-
cial and discriminating laws.

Dog owners affected by unjust laws have joined ranks in
the courtroom to appeal in several instances against a series
of legal test cases. The courts' decisions are contradictory,
but the majority of judgements have been in favour of the
dog owners. At present, legal proceedings are pending at the
'Bundesverfassunggericht' (Federal Constitutional Court)
and the 'Bundesverwaltungsgericht' (Federal Administrative
Court). The dog owners hope that these two high courts
will finally rectify this situation.

THE ANTI-DOG 'VIRUS'

To clear up any misunderstandings, political opportunism isn't
limited to Germany. In almost every European country there are
politicians who feel the necessity to do something. We have to
take it for granted that this anti-dog virus is alive and well in
every European country. Secret details available to me would
blow apart the cover of this book if I printed them.

As just one example, let's take the Magistrates of the city
of Madrid. As part of a legislative draft, the Magistrates'
number of breeds perceived as dangerous was expanded
from thirteen to forty-seven! All of the designated breeds are
required to wear a microchip, a muzzle and to be on the
leash in public. In addition to the bull breeds, also threatened in other countries, we find on this Spanish list such
ridiculous examples as the Chow Chow, the Siberian Husky,
the Berner Sennenhund, the St Bernard, the Samoyed...!

DEFENDERS OF THE DOG
The 'Aktion zum Schutz Aller Hunderassen' (Campaign for

the Protection of All Canines) was formed to gather support and signatures for a petition to be presented to the European Parliament in Strasbourg, France. This campaign was actively supported by the WSBA, the World Society for Animal Protection, London, the 'Bund gegen Missbrauch der Tiere' (Union against Animal Abuse), 'Gesellschaft für Haustierforschung e. V.' (Domestic Animal Research Society), as well as leading German canine publishing companies and magazines. On October 26th 1999, the signatures (under petition number 389/99) were presented to the parliament's petition committee (number 58,341).

Canine supporters are petitioning that the European Parliament should intervene in all European countries, in order to achieve dual aims: that dogs are recognised as being a national cultural asset and that in all EU countries animal protection is respected and defended as a legal institution. Nicole Fontaine, the President of the European Parliament, was also asked for her help. Distinguished animal defender, Brigitte Bardot, also supported this petition. Signatures were received from 27 different countries, including such non-European countries as Australia, El Salvador, Guatemala, Canada, USA, Mexico and Russia.

The international support for this petition demonstrates on worldwide basis how threatened dog owners feel by their own politicians and the media. Now, all we can do is wait and see if the president of the EU and European Parliament's Petition Committee will accept the request of all these friends of the dog.

Chapter Eight

DEVELOPMENTAL ERRORS IN CANINE BREEDING

Have you noticed that an obvious thread runs through each chapter of this book so far: lack of knowledge, prejudice, third-party influences, underdeveloped independent thought. Why should dog breeders be completely infallible when it comes to faults such as these? Canine breeding is a hobby, at least that's what it should be. It can become a passion, then a dangerous state in which it becomes close to an obsession, but, basically, I must emphasise that the great majority of breeders are true friends to canines, ready to do anything for their four-legged companions.

BREEDING AS A HOBBY

Such hobby-breeding requires a lot of time and financial sacrifice. To define it clearly, I mean by the term 'hobby- breeding' those breeders who retain, as part of the family, one or two bitches and perhaps a male, thereafter mating them, producing puppies that meet all typical Standard requirements for the breed.

These small-scale breeders are the backbone of every pedigree canine. They guarantee their puppies' early and successful socialisation. Admittedly, the greatest successes in the breeding of purebred dogs have normally been achieved by breeders who can afford to maintain a large canine stock, which allows them to build their own bloodlines. Smaller breeders can thank these large kennels for animals upon which they can establish their own bloodlines. In order to build one's own strong bloodline, one needs more than two bitches. Such ambitious goals require long-term plans extending over many generations.

BREEDING AS A BUSINESS

Who would disagree that some people do good business out of certain dog breeds! Some breeds have enjoyed a high position on the popularity scale in their home countries over a number of years, and are thus in great demand. So, it's not surprising that such breeds attract a certain type of person. In Holland they're nicknamed 'Brot-Züchtern' (bread-breeders), for obvious reasons. The fact that, specifically, the enormous popularity of many canine breeds works to their detriment is the fault of the 'Brot-Züchtern' themselves, who are only dealing with dogs for a quick cash return.

In order to correctly estimate the scale of the problem, the leading German pedigree dog club, the 'Verband für das Deutsche Hundewesen e. V.' (The German Canine Club), which represents canine breeding in Germany, says that from a total of 500,000 puppies sold per year, only 120,000 originate from VDH club members. That's only about 24 per cent. One additional fact should be made known. According to the VDH, a total of 30,000 are German Shepherds, again 25 per cent of the yearly puppy production born under the jurisdiction of the VDH. In order to correctly judge the influence this active canine organisation has on overall canine breeding, one must not forget these figures.

We've already discussed how part of human nature is to exaggerate many things. Why should any exception be made in the case of dog breeding? The thing is – and we cannot ignore this – the art of exaggeration is usually carried out at the expense of our dogs. Often incorrigible developmental errors occur, affecting the health, life-expectancy and performance of our canine companions.

To avoid any misunderstandings, let me state that this complaint is nothing new. To prove the point, a caricature dated January 1889 and published in the English magazine *Punch*. bore the title *1889 Canine Fashion*. The German Sausage Dog, the Crocodachshund, the English Bulldog and his companions were all caricaturised with a very sharp quill! Let us be careful about making any unfounded insinuations; at that time, degenerated breeds such as these were found not only in England, but throughout the entire world! Mankind has the tendency to overdo things, and to think about the consequences, if at all, only after it is too late.

Does the same go for the situation today, in the new millennium, when dog owners have access to the most modern research and veterinary medical knowledge? We cannot ignore the fact that dog breeding is conducted conservatively and with respect for tradition. Despite this fact, active canine friends of mine continually run into barbed-wire resistance while trying to convince certain breeder colleagues that they are subjecting their dogs to permanent damage. In many local canine clubs, one still encounters the three wise monkeys: 'See no evil; hear no evil; speak no evil', and, of these, 'See no evil' is the most highly valued virtue.

'Man darf das Kind nicht mit dem Bade ausschütten' (Don't throw the baby out with the bathwater). I still follow this advice from my mother. I accept that, in the last 20 years, many things have got better. Breeders have begun to expand their knowledge and apply that knowledge. In the last hundred years, a wide range of information has become available which has worked in favour of the dog. Think of the progress made in the fields of genetics or behavioural research that has given dog-friendly humans useful knowledge that was lacking for so long. Everything must be done to transmit this information to each and every canine breeder, and then action must be taken in the light of the consequences. Our canines are not endangered only by the mass media, politicians and environmental threats. I see the most serious threat as breeders' collective inability to push through reforms that are urgently needed to trigger a new way of thinking. We can't demand that the media, politicians and fellow citizens be friendlier towards dogs when we fail to do everything in our power to do justice to the species, by integrating healthy dogs into the world.

GIANTS

It is characteristic for people to overdo things; big can't be big enough and small can't be tiny enough. *The Guinness Book of Records* has recorded the Mastiff, Zorba de la Susa, weighing 141.75kg (approximately 312 lbs) as being the heaviest dog in the world. I did not weigh him personally, but Ch. Uberacht of Namous, Crufts Winner 1988 and

1989, could certainly challenge this title and seemed, to the eye of the beholder, to be even more massive. We read in the Breed Standard: "Size is very desirable when combined with quality. Height and substance are important...".

A glance at the Standard for the giant Mastino Napoletano: "He is enormously heavy, big-boned, strong, coarse and, at the same time, possesses a majestic aura". The Great Dane Breed Standard emphasises: "He is the Apollo of all dog breeds. Males have a shoulder height of at least 80 cm and bitches at least 72 cm". No upper limit is set for the Great Dane, Mastino or Mastiff. In the show ring, the rule of thumb is: 'The bigger, the better.'

Is this a worship of giants? The fantasy or dream of people who want to have a large and strong dog on their side?

With good reason, Dr Krautwurst, the Great Dane expert, points to the fact that there is a close relationship between size and life-expectancy. He emphasises, while discussing the ability to function: "The bigger and heavier the dog is, the weaker he is. This is based upon the ever more unfavourable developmental relationship between muscle, body weight and skeletal stability".

A recent new scientific opinion interpreting Paragraph 11 of the Animal Protection Law (a ban on inhumane breeding practices) links the following serious skeletal diseases with evidence of extreme size and weight: Spondylosis, Patellar Luxation and Hip Disorder Syndrome (HD).

We discover that all overly large breeds have a low life-expectancy. The few animals that live to be eight years old are the exception.

Please note, it is not just the weight of the dog but also the height that becomes a factor. The Irish Wolfhound, the largest pedigree dog in the world, can only be reared with careful consideration of a number of specific conditions, which are subject to numerous restrictions concerning the permitted exercise of young animals. In this Standard we read: "Particular largeness including high shoulder height and corresponding body length is the goal to aim for. It is desirable that the shoulder height of males be stabilized between 81 and 86 cm".

Wolfhound specialist, Mary McBride comments: "When one sees a Wolfhound for the first time, he seems to be unbelievably big.' In the 1970s, a male Irish Wolfhound was registered by *The Guinness Book of Records* as being the biggest dog in the world, with a shoulder height of 105.4 cm. With a size like this, an observer would get a real impression of a giant canine race. But, again, massive height, like weight, exacts a heavy price from the dogs, in the form of a variety of diseases, and ultimately reduces canine life-expectancy.

All breeders should know that every dog's original ancestor is the wolf, and that the anatomical build of a running predator is rigidly specialised, providing perseverence and speed for hunting in the fight to survive. Deviations in increased or decreased size and weight are possible, thanks to a wide degree of genetic variations, but should never be pursued to the extreme because of the harm it will cause to the animal. What can a dog lover do with a large, proud dog or a tiny, fragile, miniature version that is genetically programmed, through the breeding process, to suffer a shorter lifespan and a variety of illnesses?

DWARFS

Unfortunately, in spite of the documented, much longer life-expectancy of dwarfs (Toy breeds), a similar fate awaits the dwarfs as well as the giants; basically, breeding-induced blindness and breeding-induced overexaggeration always harms the animal in the end.

The Chihuahua is the world's tiniest canine. He weighs less than 2.5 kg (5 lbs), sometimes even as little as 500 grams (1 lb). When fully grown, these dogs have a shoulder height of 13 cm (5 ins). Body length is always a little longer than shoulder height.

Let me quote the *International Encyclopedia of Canine Breeds*: "the question of health plays a big role with such a little dog that sometimes weighs only a pound. Some Chihuahuas have a non-ossified spot on the back of the head called the molera (acknowledged and confirmed according to the Breed Standard). Therefore, one must always protect the dog. It could be deadly for him to receive a blow to this spot. The Chihuahua has fragile bones and other health problems that should be paid attention to by owners, among them patellar luxation, heart disease and a tendency to develop diabetes".

Despite the attractive appearance of the Toy long-haired Chihuahua, a breed which can seem to embody the joy of living, the missing cranium cap represents a constant threat to the life of this dwarf dog. While we're dealing with the cranium, think of a Pekingese skull. The extremely shallow eye sockets threaten the constant possibility that the eyeballs could fall out of their sockets after receiving soft pressure from the side. The wide, roundly formed Pekingese cranium (well-defined zygomatic arches and a highly vaulted skull cap) is unmistakable. The previously quoted scientific research concerning 'Qualzuchten', speaks of difficult births for canines with extremely rounded heads. Furthermore, it also mentions that such dwarfed dogs tend to develop brain tumours and hydrocephalus. It refers to frequent growths projecting from the nose, long soft palates, respiratory problems, extending to breathing difficulty, disturbances in maintaining body temperature and swallowing difficulties. Researchers also pointed out that teeth are sometimes so out of line, due to an extremely undershot jaw, that the bite function of the dog is insufficient.

Once again, when we review all of the evidence concerning giants and dwarfs, it must surely confirm my opinion: Hands off the giants and extreme Toys!

BREED STANDARDS AND THEIR INTERPRETATION: PRIORITY 'BEAUTY'

'Beauty is in the eye of the beholder!' One should always bear this truism in mind when deciding to study and to try to understand the various canine Breed Standards. The Breed Standard is the blueprint for an ideal example of the particular breed. In reading through it, every reasonable individual knows that this goal is unattainable, but a breeder should attempt to come as close to the ideal as possible. As a matter of fact, very few Breed Standards precisely specify to the amateur breeder what these dogs should actually look like. An attempt to furnish, with the help of an artist, a pictorial representation according to Standard requirements, led to a wide variety of diverse drawings. It would be well worth the trouble for kennel clubs to agree on developing uniform articulation and a precise choice of words for Breed Standards.

At present, there is international agreement that veterinarians are absolutely correct in warning that certain phrases in Breed Standards will definitely result in sick dogs. I have already dealt with this theme in my discussion of giants and dwarfs. It can no longer be tolerated that Breed Standards which harm our dogs should be defined or upheld by the abritrary decisions of amateurs instead of proven documentary evidence provided by professional veterinarians.

THE BULLDOG

Let us select the prime example: the Breed Standard of the English Bulldog. I love this canine breed, not because of its anatomical deficiencies but due to its unique character, which it has carried over to a large number of other canine breeds. Allow me to quote from Professor Dr Otto Fehringer's book *Unser Hund (Our Dog)*: "He is actually beautiful in an ugly way, and may possess all the possible bad qualities that one would reject in another breed. Still, at the same time, he is a walking example of a canine's body completely wrought with shortcomings .... This squat, mid-sized, stockily built animal is really a caricature of everything that is called canine! Only, he should be blind, deaf or one-eared in order to qualify for a prize in the show ring...".

The Bulldog has been considered the British national dog since the middle of the 1800s. His character embodies highly valued national virtues, but how can one explain his anatomy?

All canine breeds were at one time created for a specific purpose, and the Bulldog was unfortunate in that his traditionally minded breeders believed that the breed must be preserved as it was originally anatomically created, which was for bull-baiting. In order to be successful at this horrible and grotesque sport, the dog had to slowly crawl towards the chosen bull, the goal being to securely bite into the bull's snout. To avoid the horns and dangerous hooves of his adversary, the Bulldog was bred to have a body that allowed his great flexibility in the elbow area and steep hindquarters to smoothly creep forward, close to the ground, his back arched and pear-shaped, so that the horns of the adversary could not get a grip. To hold on to the bull, the head of the dog needed strong jaws, strong muscles, an extremely flat, laid-back nose, so that he could still breathe while hanging on. Breeders, steeped in tradition, have worked diligently over the last 150 years, concentrating on maintaining (and, if possible, exaggerating) the physical qualities created purely for the original task, ridiculous as this may seem for a healthy dog in our time.

Since 1830, animal fights of this sort have been banned, even in England. Nowadays, in spite of this fact, the English Bulldog must conform, according to his Standard, to a display of all of these anatomical characteristics if he wants to be successful in the show ring. Crazier still, it was discovered that, in practice, ambitious breeders could misinterpret Standard guidelines to an extreme extent. Such interpretations only make the whole situation much worse. Imelda Angehrn, the dedicated Swiss Bulldog breeder, has openly and honestly shed light upon the developmental errors of this breed, by devoting an entire book to the subject. Who can wonder that she found only limited support among her fellow breeders, who were used to the grotesqueness of the breed?

Body weight that is far too heavy; gigantic heads; super-wide fronts that strongly inhibit fluidity of movement; a pelvis that almost always leads to a caesarean birth; breathing difficulties due to a nose that is far too pushed-back; undershot mouth problems: much more could be mentioned that heavily taxes the Bulldog's anatomy.

Common sense alone could help the Bulldog to become a healthy breed by weeding out and accordingly rewriting the Standards characteristics that are responsible for this damage to its health.

THE SHAR PEI

Let us now turn to the Shar Pei, a breed famous for its particularly pronounced wrinkles. Leading advertising agencies find these puppies so sweet that they would like to use them permanently in promoting their products. The canine expert, however, knows that, very recently, Shar Pei breeders were forced to 'tuck' their puppies in certain breeding lines. This was the only chance for the puppies' eyes to open and develop normally. You don't understand what 'tuck' means? Think about the staples and a stapler that you need to attach two pieces of paper to each other. Wire clips are attached to the upper part of the eye in such a way as to prevent the wrinkles in the skin from completely covering the eye.

Just imagine the skin problems that must automatically arise in conjunction with such wrinkle formation. Exaggerated breeding aims such as these have dealt a severe blow to this ancient Chinese breed.

Fortunately, this wrinkled monster grows into his folds of skin and develops from a small 'hippopotamus' into a pedigree canine. The Standard clearly states that the very luxuriant skin and loose wrinkles in the young dog must be limited to the neck and withers in the mature canine. This, basically, doesn't change any of the problems that the Shar Pei is subject to because of the presence of his exaggerated wrinkles. There are many respected researchers that classify such excessive wrinkles as a 'Qualzucht' form. The opinion voiced in 'Verbot von Qualzuchten' (Ban inhumane breeding practices) has led to demands that breeding steps be taken, "to move against the tendency to overly typical, flabby, wrinkled skin (development should not disturb bodily function). A ban for all animals who exceed the set limits."

THE MASTINO

After World War II, the Mastino Napoletano, the Sicilian fighting dog of antiquity, became popular within certain show circles, and was, for a number of years, the favourite among Molosser Breeds in Germany. The number of people attracted to this breed grew dramatically, and the breed became more an object of prestige than a companion. For me, the Mastino is a prime example of how a Breed Standard's goals should not be achieved. Mastino clubs unified themselves throughout the world to form an 'Atimana'. Dr Sherilyn Allen, vice-president of this organisation, addressed the problems existing in this breed in a sensational article which generated much controversy. I quote: "The desired Mastino type is differentiated from what one would expect from other breeds. In body, form, and character, the ideal type is in direct opposition to what modern society would consider to be normal and healthy."

Dr Allen asks "to what extent do genetics affect, instead of the environment, the health of the Mastino Napoletano?" Questionnaires were distributed to all Atimana clubs, in order to research the state of health of the Mastino. The poll elicited a long list of physical problems, particularly skin disturbances, hip disorder syndrome (HD), elbow mutation, missing teeth, eczema, dry eyes with damage to the corona, flabby skin and ligaments, thickness of the elbow and rear joints, heart disease, torn ligaments, growth problems, paralysis in conjunction with growth, sterility, thyroid disfunction, dwarfs with crooked legs and outwardly turned front paws, osteochondrosis, dermoid cysts, rear-leg paralysis in young animals between four and six months .... The researcher came to the conclusion that breeders should, at best, 'use the hyphothesis that the results are genetic'.

What a shocking image for a canine friend! However, the way Mastino breeders have openly responded, and have dealt with the problems, must be emphasised and explicitly praised. Such an open discussion is generally avoided in the far-reaching spheres of pedigree dog breeding. Dicussion of developmental errors is silenced and a certain amount of courage is required to publicise the results of such a questionnaire. Here, too, one should ask: when will Breed Standards be reworked? Will the health of the animals be given top priority? Will exaggerated breeding in relation to mass and substance be corrected in favour of anatomical functionality?

HAIRLESS BREEDS

Hairless breeds especially are under aggressive attack as being victims of inhumane breeding practices. It is known that these special hairless dogs, due to a genetic mutation, occur in litters whose parent animals have fur. Very early reports exist in Africa, the Middle East, India, Turkey, Ceylon, Malaysia and various parts of South and Central

America about this breed. Originally these dogs, born without fur, were kept because of their strangeness. Mexican Indian tribes in particular cultivated this canine breed.

The Chinese Crested is a particularly old breed. In China, it is documented as having existed as early as the 13th century. Later, it arrived in England, Europe and the USA. The state of the health of this breed, target of many attacks, is judged by experts such as cynologists Anne Rodgers Clark and Andrew H. Brace: "Generally, the breed is quite robust, which is not surprising when one thinks of how many hundreds of years it has survived. Sometimes these hairless specimens are born with dental deficiencies and missing claws; this is in conjunction with the genetic factor for hairlessness. Breeders are working to better these qualities, and nowadays many Chinese Cresteds are born with a full set of teeth and claws."

In 'Verbot von Qualzuchten' (Ban inhumane breeding practices), we read about "defective hairless mutations" ... "The dogs have a very sensitive skin (sunburn, injuries, flea infestation in the summer, allergies) and show disturbances in adapting to climate changes." The resolution proposed by the commission suggested "a ban for all carriers of the defective gene".

This suggestion is certainly capable of interpretation to be acceptable. As stated earlier by our cynologistical experts, breeders are continuing to attempt to bring developmental errors under control. However, the fact cannot be overlooked that this is a very old canine breed, and we should respect it as such, as being a part of a cultural heritage! This dog has been bred over the years to be a family pet. I again quote our canine experts: "The breed has hardly any bad habits, and has elevated itself from a 'freak of nature' to a valued family member." It is particularly to be emphasised that people with allergies have no problems living with this dog.

THE GERMAN SHEPHERD STANDARD

When we discuss the results of inhumane breeding practices, we must look carefully into and thoroughly analyse the health problems of each individual breed. We must demand that no limits be set and that the health of our dogs remains our number one priority. It is extremely urgent that all pedigree Standards be thoroughly checked, so that no Qualification Standard be adopted which is detrimental to health.

Not only should there be animal protection clauses in the exemplary Standards, but all Standards should be changed or deleted after working in close conjunction with professional veterinarians and taking their advice.

Allow me here to add a few comments about the German Shepherd, Germany's most popular pedigree dog: remember that 25 per cent of all dogs registered with the VDH (The German Canine Club) belong to this breed.

Discussion of this breed has at times been extraordinarily heated, and resulted in the following statement from Dr Helmut Raiser, the German Shepherd specialist: "Hinten Frosch, vorne Hund!" (A frog from the rear, a dog from the front!). This expert's criticism was strongly aimed at extreme breeding practices. But the discussion also has to do with massive health problems. Dr Raiser maintains that 90 per cent of all Shepherds have eventual problems with their hindquarters, particularly involving Cauda equina and Spondylosis.

The fact is that, for more than 100 years, this canine breed has earned worldwide renown, and has become one of the most popular breeds in the world, top of the popularity list in many countries. The breed's triumphant march as a working dog is unchallenged, and there is certainly good reason why a quarter of all pedigree dogs born in Germany are German Shepherds.

Please let me make a few general comments! The declared goal of this dedicated breeding club is, as it has been from the beginning, to breed a working dog. Observing herding dogs worldwide, we won't find one single example of a herding dog whose back is as long as a German Shepherd's.

Herding dogs from other countries, above all from England, Holland, Belgium and Australia are visually closer to their ancestor, the wolf; a little longer than their height, short back, no overexaggerated angulation, and it is proven that the wolf's anatomy allows him to cover huge distances with almost no sign of fatigue.

I don't understand the function, in a working dog, of the elongated body of the German Shepherd, a moderately long back, followed by strong, wide loins, then a long and slightly sloping (approximately 23 degrees to the horizontal) rump. The ability to move easily is the downright gospel of the Breed Standard, built upon the supposition that a herding dog completes most of his work while trotting.

However, I have observed very many herding dogs at work in Germany, as in other countries, but only in the fewest number of cases did they perform their work trotting; more often than not, the gallop was predominant. At present, there is absolutely no physical proof that an elongated canine back would be better for a herding dog, or, for that matter, for any working dog, than the short back of his relatives in other countries and of his ancestor, the wolf.

The German Shepherd Breed Standard correctly states that any tendency to overangulation of the hindquarters diminishes stability and endurance and thus working ability. The realisation of this goal seems to pose great difficulty for German Shepherd breeders. Why else make the statement: a frog from the rear, a dog from the front?

Anatomical comparisons between the German Shepherds that actually stood before Rittmeister von Stephanitz at the time of the Standard's conception and modern show dogs, show that the Belgian Malinois looks much more similar to the original German Shepherd than representatives of the breed do today.

Active canine performance athletes uniformly demonstrate that the German Shepherd can no longer compete with the herding dog breeds of other countries in the new canine sports of Agility and Dog Tournaments. The German Shepherd is sorely lacking in flexibility, jumping strength, speed and health! The previously mentioned Cauda syndrome is evident in up to 15 per cent of all representatives of the breed. It occurs in the connection of the last back, to the first lumbar, verterbra – which creates a bend in the back of affected animals. Dr Helmut Raiser goes a step further in claiming that 90 per cent of German Shepherds are damaged in the loin ligament area, due to a narrowing of the spinal vertebra at the designated point.

Praise should be given, though, to the extent that the 'Verein für Deutsche Schaferhunde (SV)' (The National German Shepherd Club) is waging war on hip dysplasia in the breed. It's not as if individuals in the upper levels are unaware or unconcerned about these health problems. The problem is how to fully address the subject, raising, as it does, the possibility that perhaps the entire anatomy of this canine breed is in need of correction in order to be useful as a service and working dog, adaptable to many different situations, and capable of being able to continue to compete in the future.

My interpretation of the situation is that breeding practices designed solely to achieve successes in dog shows have resulted in an internal division within the Club, with beauty judges here, performance athletes there. How can such a division deal with the breeding aim of creating a viable working dog breed?

DOG SHOWS: BREEDERS' BEST OR VANITY FAIR?

Various canine breeding clubs around the world emphasise that dog shows have no goal other than to find the finest dogs of each breed, advance them and, in a planned strategy, use them for breeding purposes, thus bettering the breed. A second goal exists, unequivocally and correctly; to introduce the wide gamut of canine breeds to the public at large. These dog shows offer the dog lover a unique opportunity to personally get to know a large variety of interesting canine breeds, and to speak to the breeders in order to form an individual opinion about which dog would be the best choice. In addition, and thankfully, dog shows have recently developed the tendency to show the public not only the beauty of the various breeds, but also to demonstrate the endurance of our dogs in an assortment of performances and demonstrations.

'Ein Schelm, wer Boses dabei denkt!' (Anyone thinking poorly of my intentions is a rogue!). In order to set this straight, for more than 35 years of my life I have actively taken part in the dog show scene, as a breeder, exhibitor, and also, for more than 10 years, as a specialist judge. I am familiar with what happens in the ring. Judges carry the ultimate responsibility for dog show activities. Dog shows are dependent upon judges' knowledge and integrity to actually select and award the best dog in each breed.

However, a big handicap exists from the very beginning; all Breed Standards describe not only the anatomy, but also the typical character, of the dog, and anyone who has ever participated in a show, or has merely attended as a regular visitor, will agree that judgement of canine character in the show ring is extremely difficult. Perhaps I should mention at this point that, unfortunately, the majority of judges consider anatomy foremost and character to a lesser degree. How else can one explain why it sometimes happens that aggressive, frightened, and even shy dogs are placed in the highest positions?

It is clear that Champion canines have considerably higher chances of being bred from more often, and the majority of dog owners are surely of the opinion that good character, necessary for a reasonable life between human and canine, should have an absolute priority. For this reason, many breeders' clubs have recognised that the decision to breed should not be based solely upon show appraisals, and thus they conduct their own examinations for permission to breed. As part of this examination, anatomical merits and faults are documented, but they must also be supplemented by a concise examination of character. Such breed examination events also offer, importantly, the chance to request and examine necessary documents attesting to the absence of genetic faults. In addition, the inexperienced breeder is given the opportunity to have experts analyse the papers of the dog to be bred. These experts can specifically advise the novice breeder as to which lines will strengthen his breeding and which should be absolutely avoided. I truly believe that this sort of examination, in advance of granting permission to breed, is a far better source of effective guidance than an out-and-out beauty pageant.

Many dog show visitors must surely be reminded of the Miss Germany or Miss World beauty competitions when they approach the main ring and watch contestants from different breeds and, finally, the Best in Show competition. Many canine experts reject, with good reason, such a comparison, questioning how one can stand a Chihuahua, an

Irish Wolfhound and a Pointer next to each other and then decide which breed is the best dog in the show. The all-round judge answers: the placing is determined by which canine comes closest to his own Breed Standard.

To be honest, I admire such cynological experts; they have to keep straight in their brains (without a computer) the breed characteristics of approximately 340 of the FCI- (Fédération Cynologique Internationale) recognised canine breeds. And they must do this so perfectly that each individual breed representative can be fairly judged as to how close he comes to his ideal image, each time he appears in a show. An impressive judging achievement!

But what does the term Best in Show (BIS) really mean? Wouldn't it be much better to publicly award a dog with the healthiest anatomy, the sweetest disposition for the dog lover, and catalogue those dogs that are free of any genetic defect? Canine organisations should address priorities such as these, and spend less time on the question of how exactly the individual animals correspond to the (sometimes quite dubious) Standard guidelines.

HOW NOT TO PROCEED

An example of how not to proceed arose at the World Champion Dog Show 1996 in Vienna and Budapest. The Champion of the FCI Group IV was France's Basset Hound 'Like Daddy do Sete Moinhos'. The same dog then ranked third in the competition for Best in Show!

Please don't misunderstand me. I like Basset Hounds; their character has made them particularly special family pets and they were the selected breed of my friend Ullrich Klever, an excellent canine expert. Still, when one considers the public impact of a top Champion in a World Champion Show, then surely the message communicated to the public at large is that this is one of the most beautiful dogs of the world. Look at the Bassett Hound as a breed from this perspective. In the previously quoted document dated June 2nd, 1999, calling for a ban on inhumane breeding practices, this breed is ranked as belonging to chondrodysplastic canines. Chondrodysplasy means "the state in which the length of the shin leg bones are inappropriately dwarflike, shortened by an imbalance of the enchondral ossification with an early halt in growth of the extremities probably due to a hormone imbalance that affects the CA and P metabolism". The document's recommendation states: "Animals with long straight backs and extremely shortened legs often tend to discopathy. Therefore, breeding goals should strive to work against these characteristics in order to avoid an overtypification".

Now, a feature of the Basset Hound is not only the extreme short-leggedness, but also the completely disproportionate canine body that almost drags on the ground. Massive wrinkle development is also an additional feature of this breed, as well as the overly heavy flaps (ears) that make healthy eye development impossible.

And such a breed is chosen as one of the world's three most beautiful dogs?

In context with this and just to round off the overall picture, let me introduce the example of the Shorthaired Dachshund. This breed is also mentioned as a typical example of chondrodysplasy. The breed's extreme body length sometimes reminds me of a steamship hull. Then we read in the Standard that this canine must be encouraged to, and be able to, do strenuous work under the ground. That, in spite of the shortness of the dog's legs in relation to the length of the body, he must not move in a crippled or clumsy way, or be handicapped in his ability to move. And then just try sending this Dachshund into a rabbit hole!

Again, don't get me wrong; Dachshunds can be particularly stimulating and enjoyable family pets, but we must surely not judge them at dog shows, in their exaggerated form, as the most beautiful canine.

Shall I put forward a final example? At Crufts Dog Show 1999, the largest dog show in the world, a Yorkshire Terrier was chosen as the best canine in the show! Did the judges consider what impression this miniature animal makes on the average dog owner? I remember that, in a European Champion Dog Show in Germany, such a decision was greeted with boos.

The matter simply has to do with the public impression that results from such a decision. By chance, I personally happen to know the breeder of the Crufts Champion, and have had the opportunity to view his dogs at his home. The dogs were kept in wire cages, with wire bottoms, to protect their beautiful fur. The dogs were in cages similar to those of battery hens throughout Europe, although, admittedly, the single cages were large enough for the dogs to move about. So the Champion had certain privileges, in comparison to the average EU chicken! What I found particularly attractive were the haircurlers, single strands of hair wrapped around silk paper and fixed with a strong rubber band, the so-called 'cracker'. By the use of crackers, the flowing, floor-length hair was pinned up so that it would never break, thus maintaining its full beauty. Free play and terrier-typical romping around are strictly forbidden; they would damage the dog's beauty.

This is the price these little dogs pay for their prizes in the ring. The Yorkshire Terrier is now a dog for hairdressers, for people that have extra hours per day to take care of their precious dog's fur. And something like this is the most beautiful canine at Crufts, the world's greatest dog show? The calling-card of British dog breeding?

I would like to identify two additional examples of breed characteristics that, while being terribly irritating, are at the same time absolutely necessary for winning in the ring.

Consider the American Cocker Spaniel, thinking carefully of the consequences of those extremely long and heavy ears in daily life. In the case of the Yorkshire Terrier, the original breed was a quick little hunting terrier. The American Cocker was originally a rummaging dog that had to go through thick and thin undergrowth to frighten wildlife out of hiding. Just try letting today's American Cocker work through some undergrowth! What would his ears look like afterwards? Try to imagine how this poor show-winning dog can eat without his ears hanging in his food dish. Yes, you have guessed correctly. Dogs with long ears usually have to have them tied above their heads, or held back with a headband, before being able to eat. What a wonderful life for a dog!

Now, think about the Maltese Terrier, certainly a charming breed for fans of stuffed animals. They have such soulful eyes. But then think how many problems such luxurious fur can bring with it on a daily basis.

There are, thank goodness, only a few show days per year, but there are very many days, weeks and months at home, where it is very difficult to control such an abundance of fur. If the hair is not bound above his eyes, the poor dog can't see at all. He shares this fate with a whole series of other canine breeds richly endowed with hair, for example, the Bobtail or Old English Sheepdog. Researchers have almost pleaded with responsible dog breeders to refrain from such fashionable extravagances, because such a heavy coat considerably diminishes the dog's ability to see. But fashion still reigns supreme!

JUDGES, CAMPAIGNS AND HANDLERS

Bear with me. I'd like to comment a little further on the subject of a show's most beautiful canine, and the qualifications for all-round competition.

On the morning before one of the World Champion Shows in Dortmund, a pioneer of Mastino Napoletano breeders in Germany led his two Mastini in the direction of the event's entrance. There, he was confronted by two well-dressed gentelmen who, referring to the dogs, enquired as to what breed they were. Promptly, the proud answer came: "Mastino Napoletano!". One of the gentlemen winced in surprise and saidlamely, "Oh, God! I have to judge them today!".

Here's another example, from an international canine show in Kiel. I followed the judging of the Bull Terrier with much interest, as I was for many years a specialist judge in this breed, and I was astounded at the dog selected as Breed's Best of Breed. If I had been judging those dogs, this particular example of the breed would have received not much more than a 'very good' rating. So I was even more flabbergasted when this particular dog was finally selected as the Best Terrier and thus placed in the finals for the most beautiful dog in the show. My amazement knew no bounds when that particular dog was chosen as Best in Show!

The judge, upon an inquiry as to why he had selected that dog as BIS against the very heavy competition of experienced canine Champions, answered with the friendly remark: "The dog had such a charming personality!". This decision was joyfully greeted by all dog lovers who most value a dog's character, but it stood with difficulty, in the face of the regulations governing such final selections.

Finally, a look to the USA for a last word on the subject of the dog show. Dog owners' ambitions here extend far beyond the placing of 'Best in Show'. There is a rating list that ranges over all the different breeds of dogs. According to this, one aims for all of the Wins over the entire show year in all parts of the United States. The ambitious goal is to belong to the Top Ten Nationally Ranked dogs. It's not unusual for competitors for this crown to show in Dallas on Saturday, and then in Los Angeles on Sunday. Hundreds and thousands of dollars are spent each year on 'campaigning'. An owner needs a professional handler, press campaigns are initiated in canine magazines and trips are taken that cover the entire country. Such expenses are prohibitive for even the most wealthy of dog owners. This leads to a search for 'backers', wealthy dog lovers who agree to finance the expenses and thereby become partial owners of the canine Champion.

Professional handlers are usually responsible for more than one dog at a time, and they organise air travel with the dogs throughout the country. Their services are paid for with a daily-rate showing fee, plus a special bonus for a top placing. This is in addition to grooming fees, kennel fees, training fees, fees for picking up or bringing a dog to the airport. All this is essential to campaign your dog. Full-page colour advertisements in canine magazines can cost over $1,000 – but all of this is necessary to create a star.

Miss America, Miss World, Top Canine Placement in the National Ranking; what's the difference? But don't forget Developmental Disturbances in Show Character – a prime example of where overly active 'dog-show mania' can lead us.

EUROPEAN COUNCIL BREEDING RECOMMENDATIONS

Sometimes it is necessary for politicians and lawmakers to take action; for example, when it comes to protecting the domestic pet from excessive breeding extremes. The interesting fact in this context is that the 'Verband für das Deutsche Hundewesen e. V.' (The German Canine Club), together with numerous animal protection organisations, has for years demanded an animal protection law which would encompass all canine breeders, organised and unorganised, and require them to adhere to binding rules. Discussions concerning this proposal are currently underway. It would be very desirable for the good of our pets if lawmakers, animal protectors and professional canine experts can work together to reach agreement on this matter.

On a European level, an agreement dating from 1995 exists concerning the protection of domestic pets. This European Council resolution goes quite far, and should institute a series of arrangements that will be very difficult to improve on.

The esteemed Swiss cynologist, Dr Hans Räber, has summarised the regulations in his book, 'Vom Wolf zum Rassehund' (From the Wolf to the Pedigree Dog):

- Upper limits for large and minimum limits for small canine breeds in order to prevent skeletal and joint damage (hip and elbow dysplasia), patellar luxation, open fontanelles and collapse of the trachae.
- Set maximum values in relationship between shoulder height and body length (for example in the Dachshund and Basset Hound), to prevent changes in the spinal cord.
- A fixed minimum nose length in Bulldogs, King Charles Spaniels, Japanese Chins, Mops and Pekingese.
- A ban on abnormal limb placement: for example, 'chair-leggedness' in the Chow Chow; too-straight hindquarters in the Norwegian Buhund, Swedish Lapphund and Finnish Spitz; crooked legs in the Basset Hound, Pekingese and Shih Tzu.
- Elimination of all Standard requirements that could lead to pathological eyelid development: for example ectropion in the St Bernard, Bloodhound

and Basset Hound or entropion in various terrier breeds and in the Shar Pei.

- A ban on 'Glotzaugen' (protruding eye) in the Border Terrier, the Griffon Bruxellois, the Miniature Spaniel, etc.
- A ban on excessive ear length in the Cocker Spaniel, the Bloodhound and the Basset Hound.
- Forbid excessive wrinkle development in the Shar Pei, the Bloodhound, the Bulldog, the Pug and the Pekingese. (The Mastino Napoletano was forgotten.)
- A ban on the breeding of canines with semiletal factors (deformed tail, blue-merle, hairlessness).

The aims of the above list lie in the same general direction as those of this book; attempting to identify and bring under control, in the interest of our dogs and all dog lovers, the developmental errors present in modern canine breeding. It is naturally important that individual criteria should not be drawn up by the European Council or alienated theorists; the document of June 2nd 1999, written by seven competent experts, is just the first step. In producing the document, the authorities expect that it will certainly generate a critical reaction.

PROSPECTS FOR IMPROVEMENT

I consider that the recommendations of the European Council, as well as those of this document's board, could contribute to some improvement in canine breeding. It is important that the ethos of breeding from the standpoint of animal protection be enforced by law if necessary. It must be perfectly clear to all parties involved that the domestic dog has become Man's closest partner and companion, living with him together in 'a mixed pack'. I consider myself a liberal person who would request government intervention only reluctantly. However, the development of canine breeding over the past 50 years clearly demonstrates that certain limitations of personal freedom are necessary.

It is not enough that 25 per cent of breeders voluntarily

submit to be controlled within their organisations. This leaves the other 75 per cent of puppy producers completely uncontrolled, due to the market trade in the dogs which are then commercialised and sold. Thank goodness one is not forced to belong to a canine breeding club. An alternative exists in the introduction of basic legislative guidelines, in accordance with animal protection laws, that would give the our administrations and officers of the law the power to take action against abuse. However, an important prerequisite would be that, after enactment of the law, administration officials are required specifically to enforce these laws. I am not overly optimistic, after many experiences over the past 20 years against the background of the present German animal protection regulations.

One very important alternative cannot be overlooked; a massive public education campaign spotlighting developmental errors, thus guiding the demand for puppies towards responsible breeders who endeavour to breed healthy and sound dogs.

Chapter Nine
DEVELOPMENTAL ERRORS IN CANINE SPORT

CANINE OBEDIENCE: HOW IT WAS THEN

The 'Old-school Obedience' method of training dogs is based upon the idea of Man's absolute leadership of the pack, and the rank order of the dog in the pack. In addition to this, the concept prevailed that an owner should allow a young dog to enjoy his youth, and begin to train him, at the earliest, from about the age of nine to twelve months. From this concept of 'Dog Obedience' came hundreds of years of successful results, largely stemming from raw violence.

During all that time, on the whole, no one questioned this abusive training method. Coral collars (set with sharp pieces of coral turned inwards to inflict pain), spiked collars, slings, electric-shock collars and, in extreme cases, a hunter's punishment shot with a shotgun; all these practices were united under the idea of dog obedience, and were considered absolutely normal.

The home of modern canine behavioural research is the USA and UK, to the extent that 'English Obedience Methods' became controversial in German-speaking countries, belittled as 'Leckerlierziehung' (dog-biscuit obedience). Critics of new methods seized on the fact that modern behavioural research deals intensively with the development of the puppy from birth through the first year. However, the old-fashioned idea of continual competition for a ranking position in the 'wolf-pack' leads, in reality, to escalating absurdity. If merciless rank fighting were actually to exist in the wolf-pack, as demonstrated in 'canine Obedience' between Man and his dog, then the pack would be completely dysfunctional as a hunting unit. Co-operation between pack members would be fundamentally destroyed.

HOW IT IS NOW

Slowly, the knowledge has prevailed that dogs learn fastest and easiest when the human trainer, in parallel with the dogs' educational ability, reinforces desired behaviour with a pleasant experience, and does not stress undesirable behaviour. Eberhard Trummler, Germany's well-known behavioural researcher, once reduced the theory (for easier comprehension on the part of today's computer freaks) to the following explanation: "The puppy brain is like an unprogrammed computer. A successful programming period lasts from puppyhood to a twelve-month-old dog. The most important programming stage, affecting the rest of the dog's life, should be completed, by the age of four months, though, because the highest degree of educability exists within this time period".

In the past, these invaluable, determining learning stages were missed by dog breeders and trainers alike, thereby making the training of a dog very difficult, if not impossible. Nowadays, we know how important the role of a breeder is in influencing, for all time, a puppy's temperamental development during this early phase. Failures within the first four months of a puppy's life are very difficult, if not impossible, to correct.

Researchers have introduced another completely new discovery in canine behaviour: the dog is an extremely dependent social group animal. Each instance of isolation, particularly continual isolation in a kennel, leads to serious long-term problems. The canine is a group animal. He is dependent upon contact with his fellow canines or his people. Isolation leads to seriously disturbed behaviour, from shyness through destructive behaviour to aggression.

At this point, I must admit that many dog friends misinterpret this new knowledge. We have already tried it out with our own children as 'anti-authoritative education'. Its success is more than dubious; in fact, it is so nonsensical that our anti-authoritatively raised children are returning to forms of clear family discipline. This has nothing to do with 'prügeln' (flogging); rather, disciplined order within the family has again become very important for today's generation. The same goes for canine obedience. One canine researcher rose to preach: 'Never say no!'. This philosophy is basically mistaken, for how can we teach our four-legged friends what they can do and – equally – what we don't want?

Luckily, modern dog obedience is specifically designed to motivate the dog through praise, and to continue strengthening this motivation. If a dog's actions are ignored by the 'rudelchef' (leader of the pack), then they will be abandoned after some time.

It sounds so easy, but it is worth every dog owner's while to deal thoroughly with the theme of correct canine motivation. All owners will be immensely surprised at what general achievements they can demand of their dogs, if only they learn to train accordingly.

I would like to comment again on the completely outdated idea of allowing a young dog to 'enjoy his youth'. If a dog owner, upon receiving the puppy from the breeder, methodically trains him, according to his ability to learn, then he can have a dog, at the age of six months, that is on his side and that he can take anywhere, even without a leash, because the animal has learned how to act as a well-behaved dog should.

Sometimes the process can take up to nine months because different breeds vary considerably in their ability to learn and to concentrate. However, early education is the basis for a harmonious life together within the family, and within the community, and is a absolute prerequisite for the acceptance of our dogs by society at large.

Just one more additional comment! Education and working together with the dog are the basic requirements for any 'natural' maintenance of a canine. A dog that is locked in his kennel, or ignored within the family, is not able to live a meaningful life. Dogs need to have constant dialogue with their people, doing things and sharing experiences with their 'pack' partner. Chained dogs, kennelled dogs and 'couch potatoes' all lead an unnatural lifestyle, although the couch potato, as isolated as he may seem, has the best 'deal' of the three. However, even he can become destructive due to boredom or, as a result of neglect, the result being a seemingly unwieldy member of the family.

TRADITIONAL CANINE SPORTS

Schutzhund, Protection and Security Dogs

Over thousands of years, one of the most important services our canines have given us is the guarantee of a certain degree of protection. This desired behaviour on the part of Man has its roots in territorial behaviour in connection with the development of the pack. Every individual in the pack makes sure that he defends his own territory and the other pack members. This protective function is probably one of the very first reasons why the dog was domesticated by Man.

For hundreds of years, society has recognised the natural role of the canine in protecting house, farm, belongings and people. Dogs who didn't fulfil this function were considered worthless mutts, or, if they were 'lucky', they fell into a life of ease as the lapdogs of elegant ladies.

At the beginning of the 20th century, humans discovered the increasing versatility of the canine in law enforcement and the military, again in the role of the protector. In particular, German-speaking countries developed a movement towards the police dog, the service dog and the protection dog. The recognition of the purebred dog as a 'Gebrauchshund' (working canine) became a widely popular goal of breeders in many pedigree breed clubs. At the top of the list was the German Shepherd Dog, and I certainly do not exaggerate in emphasising the impressive achievements of this breed as a protector, service and police dog; achievements that catapulted him to worldwide popularity. Today, the German Shepherd comes high (if not in first place) on the popularity scale in the majority of countries that breed dogs. This fact proves that, even today, Man still wants the dog as a protector of himself and his property.

For over one hundred years, the sport of Schutzhund has been cultivated in many countries around the world. Major national and international events annually draw a very large and passionate public following. Top achievement in working canine sport is the calling card of the successful canine athlete. The demanding profile of the sport of Schutzhund requires trail-following, subordination, trail discipline, and a wide, varied programme designed to educate the reliable canine.

Anyone who has attempted to train dogs in tracking knows how many hours of personal training in wind and weather are needed to school a dog in this discipline. If you have guided your own dog in tracking, and have achieved a degree of success, you will always harness up your dog with pleasure.

Luckily, positive motivation dominates submission training these days and it leads to astounding successes. There is no finer image of teamwork than a dog working joyfully at the side of his handler. It is obvious that they have grown together as a real team. Many hours of training lie behind such an image and, thankfully, this training employs methods that are fun for the dog as well as the owner.

'Mannarbeit' (protection work), correctly applied, is certainly the crowning glory of a successful canine education. Nowhere else is a dog required to possess more discipline than in 'Schutzdienst' (trail discipline). The goal of this discipline is to have a dog that is one-hundred-per-cent reliable as a protector, and completely obedient to his handler. The working dog is at no time allowed to use his bite without a specific order from his handler.

The use of bite is, quite rightly, a much criticised point. Ask an experienced canine Obedience trainer how many of the dogs registered in this discipline actually pass the final examination. At best, it is about 20 per cent, more often than not a mere 10 per cent, and the most rigorous examination is always in 'Schutzdienst' (trial discipline), which has the highest quota of failures.

A closer look at the facts leads to the conclusion that at least two-thirds of all dogs trained in trial discipline are not under the complete control of their handler. This is why I acknowledge a dangerous development in this canine sport. The domestic dog inherited from his ancestor, the wolf, a natural shyness of Man. In the wilderness, encounters between humans and wolves usually result in the hasty retreat of the wolf. But active participants at canine education centres know how young dogs are systematically trained with 'Ringhetze' (baiting discipline) to ignore their natural inhibition over biting a human. The object is to reinforce their confidence that it is actually acceptable to bite people.

This behaviour modification is necessary in order for a canine to be trained to become a schutzhund.

However, what happens when more than two-thirds of these dogs, after having learned to ignore their bite inhibitions, do not complete the training which would qualify them as a reliable schutzhund? Active members of Schutzhund organisations get rid of such dogs, because they have no chance of being able to compete in their chosen sport. Many dog lovers discontinue training and take their dog home – a dog who has learned to bite but failed in the absolutely essential accompanying obedience. We must recognise the latent danger in each of these dogs.

In spite of constantly rising crime, the modern public has shown very little understanding that a dog can be used as a defensive weapon. The watchdog has also lost his authority. People regard him more as a danger to society than his master's helper.

The anti-dog lobby points out other possibilities available to people for protection of themselves and their property, exaggerating the dangers that could occur with these dogs.

In such a climate nowadays, it is very difficult to communicate to the general public that clubs for working dog breeds exist, and require the possession of a successful Schutzhund qualification as a prerequisite for active breeding. Objections by private citizens have recently been made, including protests against the right of club members' dogs to attack people, even under the category of 'beutetrieb' (hunting instinct). These protestors demand (with a certain degree of justification) that the human body be protected from canine teeth.

In this context, it is true that a large number of countries allow this particular canine sport to exist only in a very limited form, instead encouraging the enormously popular 'Obedience', a very varied examination of aspects of obedience and subordination. These countries avoid the 'schutzdienst' discipline.

Even in Germany, the homeland of working dog sport, there are relatively few clubs which include the training of schutzhunds in their education programme. New, exciting opportunities for 'team dog/man' are becoming more and more popular (see more in Chapter Eleven on dogs as leisure-time companions).

If working dog sport is to be actively continued in its present form, with the support of the general public, then the organisations concerned must start thinking about how to considerably limit membership. It is especially important to address the problem of what to do with dogs that are partially trained, but unreliable as a schutzhund. Let us not deceive ourselves; the question of human safety is a central public concern and, without a solution to this problem, dog lovers will continue to give the press and media the opportunity to spread a justified fear of our dogs.

Sighthounds

Dedicated journalist Renate Nimtz-Koster triggered horror and protest across Europe in her shocking 1997 *Spiegel* report *The Sprinters' Slave Market*. I quote: "Drowned, abandoned, put to death: after a short racing career, thousands of Irish Greyhounds, the canine thoroughbreds, are yearly 'sorted out', or bartered off to Spain, where they die miserably. Mass breeding practices are even financed by EU subventions, to the detriment of the animals."

This is indeed the situation, the grim truth. There is an Irish Greyhound industry that produces the largest number of Greyhounds worldwide, and exports them all over the world. Yearly production numbers average around 20,000 registered Greyhounds. Approximately 5,000 of these are weeded out each year and designated as unsuitable for the 'sport'. Thousands suffer this fate as young dogs, the rest after a short, unsuccessful racing career or after suffering 'sport'-related injuries. "The animals that suffer a quick death by the needle are the lucky ones," says Marion Fitzgibbon, President of the ISPCA, the Irish animal protection agency, adding that "a Greyhound that fails loses his life." A cheaper way for these animal 'friends' to get rid of the surplus dogs is by drowning them, tying a cement sack around their necks after having first cut off ears tattooed with registration numbers, thus masking the identity of the owners. In Ireland, there are various auction houses that sell off discarded Greyhounds cheaply to Spanish buyers. The fate of these animals is factory-style kennels, and wear and tear in the heat of Spain's racetracks.

After having done their duty in Spain, these poor dogs will be hung up on trees by their necks or rear legs, as documented in Valencia. Animal protector Fermin Pérez Martin, of Medina de Combo, testifies to nearby villagers hearing the screams of the condemned dogs which, after having been strung up, would still support themselves for a while with their forelegs.

An additional scandal must at this point be brought to light. Ireland's mass dog breeding industry has been financially supported by the European Union for a considerable time. So, instead of concentrating on meat production, many Irish farmers were able to switch over to the production of canines for profit. In Brussels, a 1994 agricultural 'Untermaßnahme' (resolution) was passed, which foresaw an allowance to increase the annual export numbers of Irish Greyhounds from 10,000 to 15,000 by 1999.

Helga Fleig and Ursula Keller initiated, together with the support of animal protection agencies, breeding clubs and canine magazines, a petition against this financial support from the European Union. A total of 31,450 signatures were collected within a few months and were presented to the EU on May 6th 1998.

The EU Commission, in a letter dated June 25th 1998, informed them that "the European Union's subventioning of the breeding of Irish Greyhounds was, in the meantime, withdrawn".

This is an excellent example of how private initiative can improve the fate of the animals, even in our modern world. However, we all must be clearly aware that the horror of Sighthound racing continues without extra help from the European Commission.

The races, fed by the passion to gamble, take place on racetracks that are in no way designed for a dog's anatomy. The animals' ligaments and joints suffer serious injuries, which exclude them from an active racing career. The required speed of a racer averages up to 64 km/h, and every start causes great strain.

Anne Finch, founder of the UK's Retired Greyhound Trust, describes racing injuries thus: "Injuries are common to feet and legs. The dogs go round the track counter-clockwise and, as they negotiate the bends, their bodies lean inwards towards the centre of the track while their feet try to maintain equilibrium by gripping the ground. These injuries may be stresses and tears to ligaments and tendons and even fractures of the toes, wrists and hocks. Neck injuries can be incurred at the end of the race when the hare stops and the handlers have to catch the dogs."

Anne Finch's efforts and Renate Nimtz-Köster's article are largely responsible for the founding of rescue organisations for retired Greyhounds. These organisations are almost overwhelmed by, and can hardly fulfil, their many duties, due to the enormous irresponsibility at betting-orientated racetracks. In this situation, Man is the beast!

Galgos are being deliberately slaughtered in Spain, the Galgo being a Sighthound breed that Spaniards are particularly proud of. Worlds of difference lie between such national pride and the pitiful fate of these dogs! Yet, whether they are Galgos, or another Sighthound breed, there is no difference in the animals' fate if they don't bring in the desired amount of money.

Naturally, at this point it is only fair to emphasise that, in many European countries, dog races are held under different conditions. There is no betting, the main goal of the races being to give the dogs the opportunity to physically satisfy their need to run; after all, they were bred to do just that! However, injuries and long-term effects of 'wear and tear' are unavoidable, even in this kind of 'tame racing'.

Here is the nub of the issue! Sighthounds, like all canine breeds, were bred for a specific task. This task, the hunting and pursuit of wildlife, mainly rabbits, is almost extinct. However, these beautiful canine breed have been maintained, unmodified from an aesthetic viewpoint. Unfortunately, as a result, many difficult problems develop for Sighthound owners. In Sighthound circles, the opinion is that the dogs should regularly prove themselves on the racetrack, and, correspondingly, competitions are supported and held. However, the organisation Greyhounds in Need has proven that the majority of these dogs are also generally just as happy without having to race, a prerequisite for such a lifestyle being that the dogs are kept in larger groups, so that they can work off their energy in play.

In conjunction with this, I wish to stress that most of these canine breeds make extremely pleasant housepets, as long as people create opportunities to provide the necessary exercise for them. Such are the simple, natural guidelines governing the maintenance of Sighthound breeds. Anyone who cannot provide these physical requirements should turn to another breed, even though these aesthetically beautiful breeds may strongly appeal to dog lovers.

To sum up, the majority of Greyhounds, throughout the world, live in deplorable and abusive conditions, sometimes penned together in tiny kennels, their fate very similar to European Union battery hens. What human beings do to Sighthounds differs little in cruelty from to the brutal, organised dog fights of 150 years ago. A developmental error in canine sport, this must be recognised as something that is happening at Irish, English, American and Spanish racetracks.

I expect that many of us no longer view this practice as a sport, but as animal torture.

Sled dogs

Who isn't familiar with the tremendous accounts of the historic Polar researchers? "Never were dogs or men more loyal than those poor creatures," wrote Admiral Robert Peary about the dogs that helped make it to the North Pole in 1910. "Day after day they struggled across the frightening frost-crusted, icy desert, fighting for their and our lives. Working day by day, they gave every ounce of their strength and then fell soundlessly in their tracks, as if dead."

Polar research at that time ended in the North with Peary's triumph and with researcher Roald Amundsen's achieved goal in the South, but both teams would have failed without the unbelievable achievements of their sled dogs! Lloyd Grossman honoured this achievement: "It was the largest combined success of Man and canine ever achieved in history, and, without the dogs' help, anything of the sort would surely have been impossible at that time!"

The tradition of heroic achievement by sled dogs was continued in the form of the well-known Serum Run of 1925, when Leonhard Seppala's sled dogs, with lead dog Balto up front, saved hundreds of Alaskan citizens from death.

Dr Curtis Welch, the only doctor in the small town of Nome, had discovered a case of diphtheria. At that time 2,000 people, mostly Eskimos who were very susceptible to the disease, lived in the town. Dr Welch expected a terrible epidemic, bacause the only supply of antitoxins were in Anchorage, 900 miles away. All possible forms of transport were eliminated due to the difficult weather conditions. The Alaskan railroad was able to transport the serum only as far as Nenana, where the railroad tracks ended. As a desperate measure, 20 sled dog teams were organised to constitute a relay from Nenana to Nome. It began on January 27th 1925 at a temperature of minus-45 degrees Celsius. The life-saving package, weighing 10 kilograms (4 lbs) was loaded on to the first sled and the journey began.

On February 2nd, at the conclusion of this treacherous canine relay, Gunnar Kasson stumbled, half-frozen, into the practice of Dr Welch, bringing the vital frozen medicine so that the vaccination process could begin.

Today, the Iditarod, the world's hardest sled dog race from Anchorage to Nome, spans a distance of over 1,100 miles and commemorates this canine feat of heroism. American sport journalist Tim Moray reports, "It's like being on another star for two weeks. Life is boring after having raced the Iditarod."

Iditarod fever is still as intense in 2001, and the race is beamed by TV broadcasts into American living rooms. A win brings high esteem to both dogs and mushers.

No wonder this example of sporting prowess by dogs has been mirrored in many European countries? Canine-enthusiast athletes have directed their attention to the sport of dog sledding, and participated in worldwide competitions. European teams now participate even in the Iditarod. The most famous European race is the Alpirod; as the name suggests, it takes place in the European Alps. Every sled dog competitor dreams of a win in the Alpirod!

As much as we admire their achievements, we must also reflect just as much on how northern canine breeds can adapt to living habits and temperature conditions elsewhere. The fact is that these dogs need an enormous amount of training and work in the summer as well as in the winter. Using self-designed training carts in summer, sled dog athletes try to keep their dogs fit year-round. A 'sled dog sport industry' has arisen to supply these canines with sports equipment, harnesses, clothing, special food and many other things.

Now, it is part of human nature that such beautiful, famous dogs should be kept by many less athletically inclined or sporty dog lovers. The friendly character of these dogs deserves to be praised, but they still have a monstrous need for physical activity. Real admirers of the breed find themselves planning daily hour-long walks, as well as mountain-hiking, in an attempt to meet the needs of their dogs.

However, the question remains, are these dogs suitable for a domestic life, far away from the snow-abundant regions where they are at home and in their element? Certainly, there is no satisfactory answer to the question of what happens to the dogs within a few years, when they are worn-out as a result of their sport-related activities. This problem was easily solved in their countries of origin. The dogs that could no longer achieve what was required of them were singled out and shot on the post. These are the same merciless rules we have already seen in the case of Greyhounds, used by people with working dogs which they exploit. Thank God there are civilized countries in which such a solution is unthinkable! Retired working dogs in these countries spend the major part of their lives in kennels. They are released to dog lovers only under special circumstances, simply because the dogs, even in retirement, demand too much from a normal dog owner.

I have spoken to many hobby breeders who have discontinued their activities, due to the unavailability of suitable buyers who could provide the amount of exercise needed by the dogs. Even enthusiastic followers of sled dog sports agree that the maintenance of these dogs in large cities is impossible and, for the majority of private owners, very difficult. This kind of sport, in spite of the enthusiasm for high athletic achievement, would be better limited to the countries in which the individual breed could be best utilised according to its talents.

Chapter Ten
DOGS IN ANIMAL RESCUE SHELTERS

It is a frightening result of our 'Wegwerfgesellschaft' (throwaway society) that dogs who have, for whatever reason, become irritating to their owners or unmanageable, end up in animal homes or rescue shelters. The whole effect of this is catastrophic for the animal, while human behaviour is reflected in a series of statistics: The 'Deutsche Tierschützbund e.V.' (German Animal Protection Agency) reports that, out of a total estimate of over 100,000 rescued canines in 1999, 40 per cent were taken in before and during the holiday period. In comparison, in 1995, the numbers of rescued dogs were still averaging around 83,700.

In 1996, 17,200 dogs were registered at 375 animal shelters belonging to the 'Deutsche Tierschützbund e.V.' (German Animal Protection Agency). These numbers are only surpassed by the number of cats, generally averaging approximately 24,000 in total. Registered numbers in 1999 were 140,000 cats, compared with 101,600 in 1995.

This is an enormous tragedy and poor reflection on the enduring myth of Germany's 'Tierliebe' (love of animals)!

REASONS WHY DOGS END UP IN SHELTERS
What are the main reasons for an animal owner to take his pet to an animal shelter? Experts Judy and Larry Elsden published, in an UK study of the subject, five clear and separate reasons why dogs become homeless:
1. Loss of owner (death, divorce, loss of home or relocation.)
2. The dog doesn't suit the owner, or the owner doesn't suit the dog.
3. Strays. An especially serious problem in England, where some dogs have never had an owner in the truest sense

of the work.

4. Defective training, in some cases canine abuse.

5. Psychological disturbances.

The most usual reasons for separation are mistaken expectations by the owner about the dog. This is based upon a lack of knowledge about what duties and responsibilities are involved in caring for a canine, little understanding of canine peculiarities and the fundamental mistake of buying a dog on a whim. The dog ends up footing the bill!

We discover a number of aberrations in, of all places, animal-friendly England. There, stray dogs are quite common and still able to multiply unchecked. The RSPCA, the most important UK animal protection organisation with many large centres distributed all over the country, reported in the 1990s that in each of its animal shelters up to 50 per cent of all dogs admitted had to be killed. We quote Judy and Larry Elsden on the subject: "You may think that the most common reason for a dog being destroyed is because it has bitten someone, or misbehaved in some other way. Actually, in the majority of cases, the crime for which a dog receives the death sentence is that it has been abandoned, lost or thrown out by its owner, and no other person can be found to take responsibility for it. Furthermore, although most rescue organisations do not take advantage of it, the law allows the dog to be destroyed if there is no claimant for it after seven days."

Other UK animal shelters speak of a death quota of up to 20 per cent. In Britain, the dogs that are most fortunate are those that find shelter in one of the welfare organisations of pedigree breed clubs. Normally, no dogs are put down in these establishments and, more than likely, the ones that are not able to find a home receive care for the rest of their lives. But the dogs are, as a result, forced to remain in kennels, a life behind bars for the rest of their lives.

PROBLEMS FACING SHELTERS

Animal protection plays an important role in British society. The Battersea Animal Shelter in London was founded in

1860. In 1888, Queen Victoria became the official patron of this shelter, and, in 1956, Queen Elizabeth II decided to continue this unbroken tradition. As is only to be expected, problems escalate quickly in an animal shelter in London. Battersea is forced to cram the rescued dogs closely together, with kennels sometimes stacked three deep. The ever-growing need for space finally led to land acquisition in the Windsor area, where homeless dogs could have a better chance of resocialisation.

Meanwhile, animal shelters in Germany are facing an extra burden due to the irrational 'Kampfhundeverordnungen' (fighting dog decrees). In a press release by the 'Deutsche Tierschützbund e.V.' (German Animal Protection Agency), we learn that approximately 1,000 'fighting dogs' have found asylum. A 1999 press release from the same organisation appeals for an end to mounting hysteria on the subject of so-called fighting dogs. We quote: "The German Animal Protection Agency, an organisation consisting of 700 Animal Protection Clubs that operate 400 animal shelters across the country, appealed to the Minister of the Interior in a strong letter. According to animal protectors, the general public has the right to be protected from truly dangerous dogs. However, prohibition of, or forced castration of, certain canine breeds is not fair to the majority of these friendly, dependable representatives of their breed, and is not even close to finding a solution to the problem."

President Wolfgang Apel made this plea: "Stop discriminating against responsible dog owners and their dogs by non-objective generalisation!" The press release concluded: "Nationwide, many animal shelters are already facing almost unsoluble problems. Even friendly, family-capable dogs of these breeds are becoming practically impossible to place in a home. The problem of so-called 'fighting dogs' has, so to speak, been dumped at the door of of the shelter's kennels. Those politically responsible then promptly disappear. Monetary help or subsidies are being cut at the same time."

AN APPEAL AGAINST THE DEATH PENALTY

In Germany and many other European countries, I have unfortunately failed to find clear statistical data specifying how many dogs per year have to be put down simply because no one wants them anymore. The situation for many animal shelters is one of threat, due to the fact that 'Stiefvater Staat' (stepfather State) has stingily administered public funds earmarked for the care of homeless dogs. Animal shelters largely have to depend upon generous donations, that are not enough to guarantee long-term safety for the animals. A remedy is urgently needed in this country.

The German Animal Protection Law specifically forbids killing animals without a definite reason; this law also, and not least, extends to actions taken by veterinarians. However, as long as it is possible to take a dog to the vet and claim that it threatened or harmed a family member, then the dog's safety is in jeopardy. How can a vet check if the owner's version of events is true or whether his motive is just to get rid of the dog.

However, we cannot talk of animal protection and animal safety as being synonymous when, for example, respected UK animal protection organisations put down the very animals they are trusted to protect, simply because financial funds are lacking to support and ensure the safety to all animals in need.

My appeal to the authorities is to financially equip animal shelters and to substantially expand legislative protection. There is no doubt that some disturbed dogs can never be successfully placed in a new home. However, this is the exception and in no way the norm. Even in the case of dogs that have a 'background', there are, according to modern researchers, extremely effective therapeutic measures that can be taken. These measures should at least be tried before the difficult decision to kill a dog is taken. Personally, I suggest a law that requires the dog under threat of death to be examined by two impartial experts. If both parties are of the same opinion, that therapy is impossible and that humans and other animals are in danger, then, and only then should the animal in question be painlessly sent to the 'everlasting hunting grounds'.

The present situation in animal shelters is insupportable. Their staff are not able to put right all the harm that mass breeding and dog owners' ignorance has done. They need lasting support from us all, including voluntary donations as well as much more help of a political nature.

Chapter Eleven
DOGS AS LEISURE COMPANIONS

Scholars agree that our society is moving more and more towards a shorter working week: therefore, leisure time is getting longer. Over a lifetime, an ever-shorter professional life means a longer retirement. As a result, growing independence from paid employment challenges Mankind to develop his own initiatives and fulfil himself in his new life. Will he always choose the right path?

A HEALTHY ALTERNATIVE

Doctors are unenthusiastic at the prospect of increased leisure time leading solely to us to spending it watching television, or adopting computers and the Internet as our foremost leisure-time partners. Some critics say that the human eye is becoming square, adapting to watching the TV or a computer screen!

Professional life may well have become shorter, on a daily or a lifetime's basis, but it has also become more stressful and demands even more from people. A variety of medical examinations reveal that people with animals, particularly dog owners, are much less susceptible to widespread illnesses of the 'civilised' world, especially heart disease and high blood pressure, and at the same time more resistant to all sorts of cold symptoms. A dog owner's daily routine automatically includes a half-hour walk before going to work. After eating, the lady of the house might take out the dog, and, when her husband comes home tired from work, an invigorating walk with his four-legged friend is exactly the right antidote to a tiring day.

I grant that life with a dog, especially the physical demands our canines make, means additional responsibility for us. Dogs want to go for walks, even when it's snowy and icy, in storm and in rain, and also in summer when it (sometimes) gets very hot. However, just ask your doctor; he will confirm that these canine needs constitute a veritable 'fountain of youth' for you. If it were possible to prescribe a dog, very many reasonable doctors would certainly do just that.

Not only physical exercise but a much more varied world of discovery opens up to us during excursions with canine companions. Dogs are very effective catalysts, and can act as the go-between which results in lifelong friendships, and even marriages.

BACK TO NATURE

Dogs and leisure time; what a worthwhile alternative to TV or computer leisure time! Looking back, how many marvellous experiences would I have missed if I had not had a dog? Just try taking an early-morning 'Pirschgang' (deer-stalking walk) through the woods and fields. Your dog will show you all the wildlife along the way. Once I stood, together with my Bullmastiff bitch, in the middle of a herd of wild sows and their piglets; we knew the animals and the animals knew us, due to the regular walks we took through the forest. I remember spectacular hour-long mountain hikes that would have been impossible for me, due to a pronounced physical handicap, without the motivation and encouragement I received from my dogs. I also recall long walks on the beach of the Isle of Sylt, with its strong surf, our Bull Terrier working hard to retrieve driftwood out of the high waves; wandering through the Lüneburger Heide; enjoying picnics in the heather: would I have ever experienced these things without the challenge from my four-legged friends to get out and experience nature? Thanks to the constant company of my dogs, I feel a great empathy towards nature, and have gained experiences that a television or computer will never be able to offer. Let us regard our dogs not only as a go-between and catalyst for human relationships, but also and primarily as a way of perceiving our environment, the forest and fields and the animals living therein! Those who have never experienced this are not qualified to enter into the discussion. And, by the way, my children were also granted, through their association with our dogs, an access to nature that has accompanied them throughout their lives.

Just one additional comment. When listening to public debate, it's easy to form the opinion that joggers and dogs don't belong together, each requiring their own space in the outdoors. This idea is definitely a completely mistaken one. Many enthusiastic joggers nowadays are accompanied by their four-legged fellow joggers, who often show more endurance than their two-legged companions. Running together is terrific fun for both human and canine! If any problems exist, then they occur only because some irresponsible dog owners do not ensure that their dogs learn correct social behaviour with joggers, so that their young dogs leave these athletic friends of nature alone.

What joy we humans experience daily with our pets! Just think, dogs are always by your side in any kind of weather, whenever it is time to get out and commune with Mother Nature!

THE DOG ON OUR SIDE

Agility

We can do nothing worse for our dogs than to leave them with nothing to do. They need to have a task, to work off their energy and to use their senses. Canines with nothing to do, lying idly on the couch or imprisoned in a kennel, can quickly become moody and destructive towards the interior décor or their kennel facilities. As we have seen in an earlier chapter, dogs are not like AIBO, nor a Tamagotchi; one cannot just switch them on or off and then leave them in the corner. They need companionship with people and want, as a member of the pack, to be challenged to pursue activity together.

How do dog and man build an team? By doing things together, taking on an interesting challenge. In Northern England, as early as 1977, dog fans first conceived a new canine sport – Agility. The first public Agility performance was staged in 1978 at Cruft's, Britain's largest dog show. To describe it simply, dog and owner run together through an obstacle course, similar to the horse show-jumping competitions we are familiar with. The obstacles are hurdles, a seesaw, a balance beam, a flexible tunnel, a slalom and a long jump. The goal in Agility is to complete the course, without missing elements or knocking down an obstacle, in the fastest possible time as a dog/human team.

So that all dogs can take part in this sport, large and small breeds compete in different divisions, and the obstacles are lowered accordingly for smaller dogs. Bull Terriers are little heavyweights and considered not particularly Obedience-orientated. But both Bull Terriers and Bulldogs show great joy as they take part in Agility. If these breeds can do it, so can your dog.

Canine Tournaments.

Adolf Kraßnigg, a dog tournament sportsman, describes this new sport as "*the* free-time experience for man and dog". Very many dog owners, who just wanted to take part in an activity with their dogs, have discovered the attraction of this new sport/discipline at their local canine club. Dogs of all sizes and breeds compete with one another. Your dog will be confronted with new problems to solve, instead of the original duties he was bred for but which are no longer required of him. Kraßnigg describes the scene at the training centres: "Lively, confident kids, eight years old or younger, are actively busy at Agility training centres or in competitions, alongside fast, ambitious teenagers and single people. And next to them are romping senior citizens, the older the better – 50 years old and not a bit rusty!"

Agility is an ideal sport for the dog owner or committed jogger who can devote himself to his own love of exercise, combined with having fun with his dog. Who knows, this canine tournament sport might eventually become an Olympic discipline! A quadrathalon of events include hurdles, slalom, obstacle races, open-field racing and a combination speed cup. Ten contestants must participate in each of the competition events. For the smallest two-legged contestants there is the elementary class, restricted to children up to 10 years of age, followed by the youth class, junior class, individual action classes and, finally, the senior class for those dog handlers more than 61 years of age. There are team, single and family events, by which strategy this canine sport attempts to provide attractive competition to include all age groups and canine breeds. Furthermore, all disciplines are held in the open air, requiring extensive training, bodily fitness and a readiness for action.

As Stig Carlson argues in this book, canine sport must become more attractive to all members of the general public, providing challenges that can compete with the variety of entertainment available to us today. Canine tournament sport is still getting started and needs careful care and publicity. However, I am sure that, especially for the young and the old, this sport can provide as great deal of fun for every spectator and each active participant. Would you like to have some of this kind of fun? Then take your dog to the nearest canine sport centre and try it for yourself! It will be worth it.

Travelling

We have already discussed the fact that our leisure-time society has greatly expanded the duration of our annual vacations. Many of us have got used to taking a vacation twice a year. Then what do you do with your dog?

There is only one answer for all those dog owners who have truly integrated their dogs into the family, so let's hear what they have to say:

"The dog comes along with us for the vacation, because that is the time when we can devote the most time to him."

"If the dog cannot come with us due to enforced hindrances, such as plane travel, quarantine restrictions overseas or sightseeing trips through overcrowded cities, then one must resort to a live-in 'dog-sitter' to soften the difficult period of absence."

I must admit that perhaps I regard the situation too optimistically. Many, far too many, dog owners have got used to finding good and reasonable kennel care, and booked early enough, so that the dog can be looked after during the period of absence. However, what an upheaval for a dog that is used to living with his family! Let me return to the topic of a holiday spent travelling together with your dog. By planning a vacation correctly, there is enough time and opportunity for children, dogs, hiking, swimming, mountain-climbing and other new experiences. Our canine family member is accustomed to being at our side during all excursions, thanks to his well-trained behaviour. He does not disturb anyone in the hotel or camping area, nor any fellow holidaymaker. I have undertaken long hikes along the beach on the beautiful island of Sylt, and extensive walks over open fields with my dogs; they particularly loved the swimming excursions, despite the saltwater!

How beautiful it was in the Lüneburger Meadow, dog at my side in the early morning, finding meadow snails and studying the familiar wildlife. Excursions on horseback, the dogs having been well trained to run beside the horses, have made for joyful holiday experiences. Family vacations really begin to be fun when our dogs can accompany us everywhere.

Allow me to make one last comment. Vacation fun can only happen with a well-behaved dog, and by taking into account a strict consideration for the interests of our fellow citizens. On Sylt Island, I remember the appreciation of an elderly lady confined to a wheelchair, who was able to pet my St Bernard bitch, Zarah, after the dog had lain her head in the woman's lap. Truly, many of our dogs can be wonderful ambassadors of their breed, especially on vacation.

Chapter Twelve
DOGS FOR ALL AGES

There is a unique book entitled *Why Children Need Animals*, written by Professor Reinhold Bergler. For years, this social-psychologist has intensively researched the question of how much influence family pets have on people, especially children.

GOOD LISTENERS

The research shows that dogs are ideal communication partners. Children of all ages speak extensively to their dog. A general summary is as follows:

Discussions with my Dog

Percentage of instances mentioned (300 interviewees)

Tell secrets	68%
Don't tell secrets	32%
Tell everything when I'm angry	61%
Conflict and anger with the family, with friends and in school	43%
Sadness and worries	20%
All good experiences, e.g. 'When I'm in love with a boy'	15%
Secrets of friends, e.g. 'When I find out things from my friends, that my parents shouldn't know about'	15%

Single Instances:
Narrations of dreams, personal aggression against others.

Reference source: Reinhold Bergler *Why Children Need Animals,* Herder Verlag Publications.

Could you have imagined how many topics of conversation children have with dogs? Or why you can trust your dog with such good secrets? Or what an excellent mediator he is when there is conflict and anger in the family, or with friends at school!

Parents and sociologists discover these facts, often, unfortunately, as a concept completely new to them. Dogs are witnesses to secrets that parents are not allowed to know, and sometimes a dog is the first to know when his young mistress has fallen in love with a boy. Professor Bergler's research about the basic relationship between children and dogs is especially important in the following table:

RELATIONSHIP BETWEEN CHILD AND DOG

Percentage of instances mentioned (from a sample of 300)

When I come home from school, my dog greets me and is happy	98%
I am happy when I play with my dog	96%
I always have many good and also funny experiences with my dog	95%
I am always happy with my dog, because he is always happy with me	95%
I can tell everything to my dog	87%
My dog is always there for me	86%
I never feel lonely when my dog is near	84%
My dog always listens to me	81%

A dog is not as mean as a person	77%
When my dog is with me I feel safe and am not afraid	76%
My dog comforts me when I am sad or have problems	74%
I feel strong when I am with my dog	70%
My dog understands me better than some grown-ups do	70%
My dog is my best friend	62%

Reference Source: Reinhold Bergler *Why Children Need Animals*, Herder Verlag Publications.

This research specifically proves what position dogs occupy for children today, and how important it is for our children to have such a life companion at their side. There are far too many 'Schlüsslekinder' (latchkey kids) who need a companion to talk to, who understands them when no parents are at home.

Unfortunately, there are also very many 'Fehlgeprägte Eltern' (mis-educated parents), who have a basic fear of dogs, learned in their own childhood. Such parents are often obsessed with hygiene, seeing it as more important than a living creature who is always there for their children and who gives them such affection. There are still parents who pull back their children, threatening: "If you don't behave, the dog will bite you!' As I have said before, many fairytales impress upon children at an early age a fear of the dog's ancestor, the wolf. Think of the examples of 'Little Red Riding Hood' and 'The Three Little Pigs'.

POSITIVE PET POWER

Professor Bergler, under the title *Dogs as Better People*, lists additional children's statements and emphasises: "A dog is not as mean as a person for 77 per cent of the children". And now a few thoughts from children themselves:

"Dogs are dependable, loyal and have time."

"Dogs don't talk back and scold."

"Dogs don't have bad moods."

"Dogs listen."

"Dogs aren't mean and sneaky."

"Dogs are honest."

"Dogs accept me the way I am."

"Dogs don't want to bring me up."

"Dogs don't constantly ask questions."

"Dogs are obedient."

"Dogs protect you."

However, be aware that the researcher noted that this 'childish indictment' continued at length and suggests that parents thoroughly mull over the facts arising from this study.

I am completely convinced that parents seriously harm their children when they close any doorways to the world around us. The dog, Man's oldest domestic pet, becomes for children a friend that they can count on and one they can trust completely. Therefore, all parents must be fully aware that, for many children, a dog is the key to understanding relationships with all animals. In him, children have a living being that unconditionally and completely trusts them, provided that they have been taught by their parents how to behave correctly with animals.

Unfortunately, the media has given many parents the idea that a dog could pose some danger for a child. This could only hold true when parents have failed to explain to their children that the dog is a living, feeling creature. However, parents must especially make clear to the dog his rank in the mixed human/canine pack, and that the wellbeing of the child is paramount. We often found that the best indication that one of our children was ill was the behaviour of our family dog. In this situation, he never fooled around; if the dog lay on the rug beside a child's bed, then that child was seriously ill. One of my Bull Terriers saved the life of our two-year-old grandchild who had fallen unseen into our pond. He pulled the child out of the water, so that the youngster could safely be retrieved by his parents. Incidents of rescued children and families happen far more often than unfortunate accidents involving dogs that are constantly served up to us by the media.

I have personal experience of the imperative need of children for animals. As a child, my closest confidant was my dog, and my heart is warmed whenever I witness an example of the completely reciprocal trust, affection and harmony between child and dog.

My hope for the future is that the majority of children in the new millennium will have the chance to grow up with a dog, to explore our environment with their pet and to find in the dog a companion for life.

DOGS AND SENIOR CITIZENS

The age pyramid at the turn of the century revealed an extreme social change in the last hundred years. The number of older people is growing steadily; we are developing into a senior society. Tremendous adaptations in the professional sector, accompanied by early physical fatigue among the working population, has led to the fact the working years of a typical lifetime work have been considerably shortened. Early retirement nowadays is the rule and not the exception. In addition, medical advances mean that average human lifespan is statistically rising year on year.

In Germany, the 'grauen Panther' (grey panthers), a senior citizens' political interest organisation, have set standards which justifiably demand rights for senior citizens. Our senior society will expand further in this new century, and it would be dreadful if older people merely find themselves sitting in front of a television or computer, having been banished to a retirement home and feeling useless.

One of the most important things for the elderly is to develop hobbies and goals for the time when careers are at an end. There are many early retirees who give up work for health reasons, but then build a whole new life. Extensive trips, taking advantage of the numerous educational opportunities available, a growing or renewed interest in nature, a possible move out of a hectic city atmosphere into a quieter area; all of these changes will become more common in the new century.

However much the new mobility of the elderly may be a cause for celebration, the inevitable deterioration in health cannot be ignored. I would like to quote Professor Dr Sylvia Greiffenhagen in her book *Animals as Therapy*: "Life is more difficult for older people than for younger people. Bodily endurance reduces considerably: what was done in no time before is now tiring and takes time. Physical attractiveness diminishes, together with physical strength. One's self-confidence sinks, and additionally, one suffers a reduction in status due to the loss of one's career. The role of the retired person leads to insecurity, and, in many people, a serious identity crisis. One compares one's goals with what one actually achieved in life. The balance of such comparisons is sometimes disadvantageous. Many of the elderly are bitter. They avoid social situations, isolate themselves until they are completely alone and cannot free themselves from this carousel of bitterness and isolation."

THE HEALING EFFECT OF CANINES

The above outline is the other aspect of our senior society, and we cannot just overlook or ignore it. The fact is that, in such situations, family pets adopt a much more meaningful position as a life companion. Elderly people who were fortunate enough to have spent their childhood with an animal have the greatest chance of benefitting from the healing effect animals can bring to human old age.

Dr Greiffenhagen highlights the most important benefits for the elderly:

1. The elderly have an increasing need for tenderness and sensitivity. The animal replaces missing human contact.
2. Animals counteract boredom. Every dog's demands on his owner force that owner to maintain a certain regularity: taking out the dog, feeding him, playing with him and taking care of him.
3. There is no such thing as fragility to an animal. A dog doesn't recognise the human ageing process, such as

slowness and clumsiness, and thus never hurts his owner/partner's pride or self-confidence.

4. The animal stimulates memory, by calling back the past and regenerating feelings that are connected to more happy life phases in the owner's past.

5. The animal helps to delay the move into an home for the elderly or a care facility as long as possible.

In our modern society, the possibility is growing stronger that older people may be allowed to bring their pets with them to the retirement or elderly home. In such a scenario, the animal could greatly bridge the difficulty of the change of environment. In many parts of the world, there are already laws in effect covering this very subject. For example, the Parliament of Monaco stated in 1990 that every old people's facility, state or private, must by law accept animals. Research reports catalogue all the advantages that animals provide in such homes. To list all of them here would fill the book.

Calculations of expected population growth in the Federal Republic of Germany estimate that the percentage of the population over 60 years of age will be 28 per cent in 2010, 31 per cent in 2020 and 38 per cent in 2030. This data reinforces the important role that dogs will play for our senior citizens in the coming decades.

Professor Erhard Olbrich, a recognised researcher into the process of ageing, notes the beneficial effects on human health that are brought about by dogs. "We know that regular exercise has a positive effect on the health of an individual. Not only the muscular-skeletal apparatus but also the joints and ligaments benefit from a swift walk. The heart and circulation system are additionally strengthened by regular exercise outdoors."

A 1990 socio-psychological study by Judith Siegel found that elderly people with a housepet were 16 per cent less likely to visit the doctor than a similar group without a housepet. However, this was especially true of dog owners who, with 21 per cent fewer visits to the doctor, were top of the list. Animal owners' usage of medication was also lower than that of non-owners.

Dogs are therapists for senior citizens! Doctors have long recognised this fact, and would like to write it on a prescription. Therefore, society's duty must be to make it realistically possible for senior citizens to live in harmony with their dogs.

Chapter Thirteen
ASSISTANCE DOGS

As an introduction to this chapter, may I again quote Professor Dr Sylvia Greiffenhagen's book *Animals as Therapy*:

"Handicapped persons, who have learned to depend on an animal's help, benefit more than simply receiving a service. The animals help them in different ways by increasing their physical activity, stabilising their identity and activating their social contact.

"From the report of a handicapped woman: 'My dog gave me the strength to be physically more active. Moreover, he gave me the ability to trust my body again, and thus improved my self-confidence and composure. My travel distances have grown farther. I am underway more often and feel less confined, and I am doing, again, what I want!'"

DOGS FOR THE HANDICAPPED

In the last 30 years, there has been an enormous change in the field of assistance dogs for the handicapped. Doctors and psychologists are discovering ever more functions for dogs as an element in therapy. Exemplary research work in the USA and UK has led to the establishment of a considerable number of training centres on a large scale, where dogs can be specifically trained for a life with, and in support of, the handicapped. The favoured breeds for these duties are the Golden Retriever, the Labrador Retriever, the German Shepherd and the Border Collie, together with other breeds that have proven their usefulness.

Although Germany is the motherland of the guide dog, German-speaking countries can only limp behind international development in this sector. Even organisations for the handicapped haven't yet fully realised what dogs could mean for their members. Our world is extremely enthusiastic about all forms of technical development, which has meant that the concept of dogs as partners for the handicapped has remained in the background for a long time, lagging behind other technical aids. Only in the last 20 years has there been a definite move in another direction.

A dog as helper for the handicapped person is seen, more and more, not only as the provider of certain services but as an especially important life partner, who helps his owner regain a place in society in spite of the handicap. In public, the assistance dog becomes a catalyst, a bond between handicapped and the able-bodied. Everything we have talked about in the cases of children and senior citizens in the previous chapter is true, in a much wider sense, for the handicapped. Anyone who has carefully observed a blind person and his guide dog, knows the tremendous faith and trust that is vital in this team. Thanks to the dog, the blind and/or physically handicapped can often be restored to a more independent life, freeing themselves from complete dependence upon carers.

The training of an assistance dog for the handicapped is very intensive and correspondingly expensive. Normally, the dogs are raised in a foster home until the age of 15 months. There they learn to interact with people and other animals and they get used to a hectic life in a large city. Finally, the dogs are taken to an educational centre where they are instructed individually. The estimated time needed to train a guide dog is approximately nine months, compared with six months for an assistance dog for the physically handicapped and three months for service dogs for the deaf or hearing-impaired.

Dogs for the handicapped, as shown by the timetable above, take a considerable amount of funding before they can actually be put to work. The average cost of a producing a good guide dog is DM 35,000; an assistance dog for the handicapped costs DM 25,000; and a service dog for the hearing-impaired costs DM 15,000. All of this at a time when administrative budgets for health projects are overburdened.

In Germany, the situation is that registered blind people

have a legal right to a guide dog, financed through the social health insurance system. As far as the rest of the handicapped are concerned, especially the enormous number of people confined to a wheelchair, a petition committee of the German Parliament ruled that the blind had a right to a guide dog and the physically handicapped to a wheelchair. This regulation completely overlooks the enormous importance dogs have for the handicapped, in supporting their personal independence and acting as a bridge to other people. This becomes even more important when one sees the additional individual services such dogs perform for the handicapped.

GUIDE DOGS

According to Sylvia Greiffenhagen's records, in Germany in 1981 there were 1,000 guide dogs per 70,000 blind people. In 1998, the ratio was 1,500 guide dogs for 130,000 blind people. Comparative numbers from the USA/Canada, are 8,000 trained guide dogs for 750,000 blind people. The great imbalance of both statistics shows how the majority of the blind are solely dependent upon the availability of technical aids. There would appear to be wilful ignorance of how the guide dog's wide range of possibilities could provide a completely new quality of life for the blind. The situation for blind citizens in all the countries of the world could be much improved if government officials saw to it that the visually handicapped were each provided with a four-legged helper and life companion.

A guide dog's achievements are amazing for every dog lover. He is able to compensate considerably for a person's inability to see, guiding sight-impaired individuals through a confusing major city such as Vienna, as is proven each year by the number of guide dogs successfully passing their examinations in the city.

Many of the sight-impaired have been able, thanks to a guide dog, to pursue their career independently. The dog guides his partner, on basis of the former's training, according to the dog's experience and following the clear directions of the blind individual. This great improvement in quality of life justifies the cost of a guide dog's education. It's high time that health insurance companies and organisations for the blind agreed to increase usage of the guide dog, combined with initiating a corresponding programme to enlighten the public on the subject.

DOGS FOR THE PHYSICALLY HANDICAPPED

To start again with the sad statistics, approximately 800,000 people in Germany are confined to a wheelchair, and fewer than 100 properly trained dogs stand by their side. Yet a dog could considerably ease a life in a wheelchair.

Long waiting lists of handicapped persons requesting a dog are reported by famous training centres in Switzerland, Austria, Holland and France. Due to the fact that the training of such dogs requires the highest degree of trainer knowledge and great sensitivity on the part of the carer, there is a long delay between the request and delivery of a dog. An additional problem, as already mentioned, is the absolute disinterest of the authorities. Just recently, in Germany, a new foundation has been created whose goal is to provide affordable guide dogs for the handicapped and to set up their own training centre.

What can a dog provide for physically handicapped people, in addition to a completely new quality of life, independence, freedom of movement, social contact and renewed self-confidence? Just imagine yourself confined to a wheelchair. Your dog could help you by ringing a bell, opening doors, operating a lift, bringing your mail, retrieving the fallen TV remote control and fetching your handkerchief. He can reach medicine, clothing and get help in an emergency. He always has time for you, doing everything he can to compensate for your lack of physical ability. However, most important of all, he is always at your side as a friend and partner, there just for you. What wonderful helper for a handicapped person!

THE HEARING-IMPAIRED

Unfortunately, we were not able to find one single dog here in Germany that has been specifically trained in an appropriate training centre to aid the lives of the hearing-impaired. In comparison, I would like to refer to the achievements of the UK programme known as Hearing Dogs for the Deaf.

Their dogs have proven far more efficient than all available technical aids. No longer does a deaf person have to stare at signal lamps and complicated electronic meters. His four-legged partner indicates the presence of important sounds and accompanies him to the source. Thanks to such canine partners, deaf mothers and housewives can again complete their chores around the house. These dogs provide additional safety outdoors because their ears are working on behalf of their deaf partner.

Dogs most suited to this kind of work are not so much those who are bodily strong as those able to alert the hearing-impaired partner to whatever might be wrong. Smaller breeds such as Terriers, Spaniels, Cavalier King Charles Spaniels, Poodles, and many others, have impressively proven themselves in this field. The fact that these small dogs are more adaptable to a metropolitan environment and don't normally require a lot of extra exercise is another advantage. There is enormous future potential in this area. Such trained dogs could greatly ease the lives of our fellow hearing-impaired citizens.

CHARITIES AND FUNDING ISSUES

Under the umbrella of charity, organisations in the UK and the USA raise the necessary finances to fund the acquisition and training of desperately-needed guide dogs. We can congratulate them, and praise the generosity and willingness to help of the majority of the population in Anglo-Saxon countries when it comes to aiding handicapped individuals. I must also emphasise the considerable part the pet food industry plays in supporting these organisations.

We have found information stands for the Guide Dogs for the Blind Association and for Dogs for the Disabled at every UK dog show. In recent years, Hearing Dogs for the Deaf have also been active in gathering public support. What a wonderful dream if we could see here in Germany a collection box shaped like a Golden Retriever on every shop counter, not only in Northern Germany, silently seeking financial aid for the disabled. I envisage the same kind of system that exists for the 'Seenotrettungsdienst' (Rescue Organisation for those in Distress at Sea)'.

Public health funding is completely overstretched, and there is little hope that things will change in the future. As a matter of fact, it's probably quite the opposite – due to the change in our population's age pyramid, costs have rocketed in this sector. Nowadays, the costs necessary to implement a major guide dog programme will have to be met by charity, industry and sponsorship in German-speaking countries as well. Fortunately, there are a number of volunteers who are doing pioneer work in this field. However, they are totally overworked and, if they don't receive any general support, they will not be able to raise the necessary funds.

We should remember that traffic accidents, natural catastrophes, illness, sports injuries and tragic genetic damage can happen to anyone. Any one of us could someday be dependent upon the help of another person. All those who are healthy should be thankful and realise how lucky they are; then think of and help those who haven't been quite so lucky.

THERAPY DOGS

The working environments of visiting service or therapy dogs are in hospitals, retirement homes, orphanages and homes for the disabled. The animals bring a welcome change to the patients' monotonous lives, reawakening sensitivity in the psychologically unstable. Many patients impatiently await every 'visiting day', having set aside a few dog treats to welcome their four-legged friends. For many patients, the dog's visit brings back memories of happy times in the past with their own dog.

In many countries over the past 20 years, a network of socially-active dog owners has been established which organises visits to the sick and the elderly. The dog owners come with their dogs to the hospital or home, knowing how important their visit is for the children, patients and aged. Patients have spoken of 'a ray of sunshine' that enters the room.

In hospitals, children's homes and homes for the aged a

'hygienic Iron Curtain' hung for many years. Modern medical knowledge (that dogs transmit far less diseases to humans than people do to other people) spread laboriously and slowly. By the way, it must be said right now that dog owners should be responsible for the health, care and cleanliness of their dogs as a matter of course.

Almost all canine breeds can be employed in this visiting role. The only prerequisite is great friendliness towards people, a desire to be petted, insensitivity to pain and self-confidence (in case a patient, due to the nature of his illness, accidentally strikes the dog or reacts with hectic movements, maybe in an aggressive manner). Visiting service organisations are careful to ensure that their members are well schooled, that their dogs are completely under control and that owners possess the necessary ability to create reciprocal fun during these visits for patients, disabled children, the aged and also the dogs.

Personal dedication on the part of the dog handlers must be high, because patients, children and the elderly must be able to regularly count on visits from a dog who has that extra 'something' which they can look forward to and care about so much. Many cases have proven that these visits are supportive of the patients' health, and that the expectation involved motivated the children, the bedridden and the elderly, giving them a new will to live.

FOUR-LEGGED PSYCHOLOGISTS

One of the pioneers in the use of therapy dogs for the mentally ill is the Bethel Health Institution in Bielefeld. An original therapeutic method was developed here in the treatment of epileptics and other emotionally and psychologically disturbed patients. The patients are given new duties that challenge them and are fun at the same time – in other words responsibility for the care and maintenance of the animals.

Paediatricians have come up with a particularly interesting form of employment for dogs. The American children's therapist, Boris Levinson, describes an animal's function of 'breaking the ice' in animal-supported therapy. He believes that the healing function of animals for people is based on a deeply-rooted need in the human soul to be near an animal:

"Animals provide half the distance on the way to early experienced warmth". For many psychologists, a high wall is built up between the human therapist and the patient that then needs to be broken through. "But an animal is useful as a 'transitional object' for the child, before he can next proceed in a later stage to a therapist, and eventually to being able to build a normal relationship with other people. This 'ice-breaker' function is successful even with autistic and schizophrenic children. Petting the animal causes relief of muscle-cramping which is a basis for the successful treatment of autistic children."

Dr Sylvia Greiffenhagen comes to a similar conclusion in her book *Animals as Therapy*: "An animal possesses the following positive effects on mentally disturbed people, according to the latest research:

1. It allows physical contact.
2. It distracts.
3. It 'speaks' and understands without words.
4. It stimulates memories.
5. It encourages bodily and mental activity.
6. It needs and gives love.
7. It rejects no one.
8. It doesn't understand illness and acts, as a result, 'normally' (whereas a human partner sends conscious or subconscious signals which could worsen the patient's disturbance.)
9. It communicates to the patient when it is treated badly.
10. It stimulates a feeling of responsibility.
12. It strengthens a feeling of self-worth.
13. It breaks through the learned and ever-growing feeling of helplessness in patients,
14. It makes a psychiatric ward seem cosy and comfortable; in this way, it betters the therapeutic climate and environment in the ward."

This expert points out, quite rightly, that the costs of keeping an animal, in comparison with what benefits they bring to the patients, are extraordinarily reasonable.

New research into the subject has revealed an astounding phenomenon; that our four-legged therapists function as a kind of 'early warning system' in predicting epileptic attacks ahead of their occurence. However, the entire area of research dealing with the use of dogs in health services is far from completed, and much more knowledge will certainly be gained in this field in the future.

Surely all of these studies show us, in an amazing way, what dogs are capable of contributing to people, healthy and ill, young and old? Can we continue to allow such achievements to be largely overlooked, while a few uncomfortable accidents occupy the spotlight, and are exaggerated by the 'anti-dog lobby'? I truly believe that our dogs have certainly earned our respect and affection, and will abundantly return these favours, if we open up all possible therapeutic opportunities to canines, for the benefit of us all.

Chapter Fourteen

SERVICE DOGS

All modern breeds of dog exist because of the fact that Mankind methodically bred them for special duties that were desirable to him. In the discussion of canines, certain members of society have completely forgotten how important this oldest domestic pet has become for us by fulfilling duties that no machine can be trusted with. The truth is that particular jobs that our dogs were once responsible for have lost their importance in the last 100 years. However, as we have seen in the previous chapters, new responsibilities have been added, which will have a growing importance in the century ahead. Dogs whose traditional functions have diminished or are now non-existent have found useful new areas of activity. It is important that breeders are fully aware of these ongoing new developments and that they contribute to this trend by methodically breeding their dogs to be capable of fulfilling their new duties.

HUNTING

Every hunter knows that success in hunting is closely connected to the quality of his hunting dog. The dog makes an ideal companion for the hunter due to his superior senses. He finds game, points to where it is, drives it toward the hunter, retrieves faithfully, and thanks to him alone, humans can pursue their quarry, helped by loud barking ultimately to find and kill the prey. German hunting law correctly requires a full-time hunting dog to be on hand for search work in every larger hunting district. Vermin prevention, hunting underground, hunting in water and in mountainous terrain; what would the hunter do without his dog?

I must admit that if we check up on all the hunting breeds that are presented to us at a dog show, and ask ourselves to what extent they are still able to carry out their original duties, we are obliged to begin to seriously doubt that hunting dog breeding has always aimed at canine hunting efficiency. Also, when we pose the critical question of exactly what percentage of hunting dogs bred annually are actually to be found working in a hunting district, then some breeds can only report a number somewhere between one and five per cent. The remaining breed members have chosen the show ring, their dogs thus becoming more leisure-time companions than hunters.

The practical use of hunting dogs is diminishing in most European countries. Larger swamplike areas and wetlands have been made dry and used for agricultural purposes, and natural wildlife preserves have been created that ban any form of hunting. However, on the other hand, we cannot overlook the fact that European agricultural politicians are, within the boundaries of overproduction restrictions, making financial help available for landowners to convert their land from a purely agricultural function to one encompassing forestry.

I am sure that very few readers of this book are familiar with the statistics on Germany's hunting season in forest and field. Here are a few figures for the 1997/98 hunting year: 406,533 hare, 1,044,809 deer, 47,655 elk, 281,886 boar, 352,094 rabbits, 502,918 wild duck, 9,965 partridge, 232,257 pheasants, 35,525 badger and 592,584 fox, to list only the most numerous prey brought down.

Without a doubt, the careful training of licensed hunters and the continual technical advances in weapons have contributed to the fact that the majority of animals shot by registered hunters are killed in such a way that no dogs are needed to seek out wounded wildlife after the first shot. However, the range of possibilities is great before the first shot – even good, experienced hunters are dependent on their dogs. The value of the annual hunting season 1997/98 was worth over 225 million DM. We owe many thanks to our dogs for a significant part of that profit.

Ever since the domestication of the canine, hunting dogs

have stood at Man's side, helping him to track down prey and, especially, ensuring that during a necessary hunt fewer animals have to suffer for long.

AGRICULTURE

When our ancestors progressed from nomadic life to the development of their own agriculture, the dog again stood helpfully at Man's side as a working dog. Wandering herds – cattle, sheep and pigs – had to be protected from two and four-legged predators. Large, defending dogs were needed for this work, to stay with the herds at all times, in all kinds of weather. They were raised together with the herd animals from the earliest age so the herd became their own pack, their territorial instinct extending to include the herd's entire grazing area. Trespassers were brought to bay or chased off.

If the humans chose not to remain on the flatlands, but to use the mountains as grazing territory for the greater part of the year, then in many countries, particularly in Spain, Portugal and Italy, there were great migrations of herds. Man needed not only guard dogs, but also smaller, agile, herding dogs, to keep the herd or flock moving, driving the beasts or keeping them together according to the wishes of their human masters.

To this day, Man has not found a better substitute for the working dedication and skill dogs bring to such work. The flourishing sheep business, the basis for wool and meat production, would be unthinkable without the dogs that take care of the flocks.

In Australia, the USA, Canada etc., domesticated animals such as sheep and cows graze gigantic territories, but let us not forget the needs of farmers in England, Scotland, France, Germany and countless other countries. Without the herding dog, sheep could only graze on meadows surrounded by fences or walls. The herding dog is capable, singlehandedly, of taking all the animals out to graze in the morning and of cleverly bringing them all home again in the evening. Such grazing would be unthinkable nowadays without the daily services of herding dogs. Think of the livestock markets that are still usual in many European countries. Here, farmers offer their animals for sale and the dog does the work of driving the herd, especially dogs similar in type to the Rottweiler.

In my youth, I lived for a time on a lonely farm; every day it was normal for a team of dogs to bring the fresh milk to the dairy. I had to get up early in the morning, in order not to be late at the delivery dock.

Yes, I admit that, today, milk is delivered directly to the dairy truck and that trucks now deliver the animals to the livestock market. We don't regularly see herds of sheep; concentration is now more on areas that are less used for agriculture. Nevertheless, the changes in agricultural politics within the EU sphere will lead to new territories, which could be forested or used by grazing animals, which will in turn need to be cared for by dogs. Already in many smaller communities, small herds of sheep can be encountered, mostly owned by amateurs who graze them, thus paying for the upkeep of their own community property.

In the USA, our old herding guard dogs have recently proven effective in the attempt to control wolves and coyotes. Sweeping programmes were reintroduced, and have clearly demonstrated that no technical method is as effective in protecting large herds as the defending canine. I can definitely imagine that, in rural regions of the future, a renaissance of the working dog is imminent – not least because well-trained herding dogs can save many extra man-hours!

One additional thing; have you ever watched Border Collies herding and looking after large flocks of geese? And ducks? These Collie types, as a result of Man's breeding, are so concentrated that they tirelessly pursue their work. These are uncomplicated dogs who excellently carry out their work of caring for our domestic animals.

There are no statistics we can refer to illustrate the advantages of herding dogs. However, the fact remains that the huge pasture industry in many countries of the world, particularly Australia, could never have grown to become what they are today without the help of herding canines. The foundation of the entire woollen industry was built upon the backs of herding dogs.

LAW ENFORCEMENT

Canines throughout the world have served as dependable helpers in law enforcement throughout the whole of the last century. These animals contributed considerably to public safety, finding work in fighting crime as well as in the pursuit of criminals, such as thieves and murderers. Thousands of police reports describe the tremendous service these police dogs provide; many policemen would have not survived without their canine partners. Valuable loot was retrieved that would never have been found without the help of the dog. Well-trained police dogs have succeeded in freeing hostages by finding their hiding places with their noses and then bringing the police to the rescue.

The nomination of 'Service Dog Breed' was the highest goal of many breeders' societies and the working dog breed committees pursued a careful breeding plan to stabilise the qualities that are needed in police work: good scent work, obedience, and innate protectiveness.

The German Shepherd became the number one police service dog worldwide. Nine breeds in all were recognised as police dogs: the German Shepherd, the Rottweiler, the Giant Schnauzer, the Malinois, the German Boxer, the Dobermann, the Bouvier des Flandres, the Airedale Terrier and the Hovavart. However, only the first four breeds are in general police use today, these being the German Shepherd, the Rottweiler, the Giant Schnauzer and the Malinois.

It is interesting to note that law enforcement duties have been expanded as a result of canine participation. In addition to fighting crime and crime prevention, we discover that part of service dog training includes a special education that can lead to specialised service dog categories of Personal Tracking Dog, Body and Missing Persons Search Dog, and Scent Comparison Search Dog. We will go into some of these new duties in depth for Customs and Rescue Dogs in the following section.

Fortunately, we have found that police-dog training has been considerably modernised over the last hundred years. Interesting parallels with overall changes in canine Obedience training are apparent, with the emphasis on a reward system and reinforcement of desired behaviour.

Hardness is also looked down upon in police Obedience training today. The foremost goal is the creation of an efficient working man/dog team.

I would like to emphasise that, to this day, Mankind has still not been able to invent anything that can in any way compete with the ability and sensitivity of a canine nose. A dog's hearing ability is also technically untouchable. The goal of every good police dog trainer is to apply the superior senses of the dog so as to assist police officers in their difficult responsibilities. The employment of police dogs in all their variety makes our world a safer place!

CUSTOMS SERVICE DOGS

The battle against drugs and the search for explosives are the responsibility of Customs departments in many countries, while, in others, these functions are delegated to the police. Successes show that in these duties, dogs are absolutely indispensable.

Anyone familiar with the worldwide drug situation knows of the untiring fight of Customs and police officers against the drug mafia, and I cannot praise highly enough the achievements of our Drug Detection Dogs. Success quotas for Drug Detection Dogs reach about 70 to 90 per cent. This means that, on a practical basis, a well-trained Drug Detection Dog can identify eight or nine out of every ten packages containing drugs. It is certain that the enormous amounts of illegal drugs existing worldwide nowadays can only be seized due to the official aid of the Drug Dog. At this point, I must refute an absolutely ridiculous rumour that trainers have to addict the dog to drugs in order to develop his ability to search for them. This speculation is entirely false.

The training of a Drug Detection Dog is in line with the familiar Obedience training methods of active reinforcement of desired behaviour. All synthetic drugs (amphetamines) have a basic ingredient detectable to the canine nose. Once the dog has learned that his partner actively rewards him when he finds the drugs, he becomes more and more enthusiastic in his work through systematic reinforcement. However, don't let this lead you to believe that such training is child's play. An instruction course in the State of Sachsen, *Advanced Training for Drug Detection*, takes eleven weeks of instruction, during which both dog and handler are transformed into specialists in this field.

The conclusion of the training includes participation in an active drug search operation in apartments, cars, air luggage and anywhere else Customs officers deem necessary. These dogs, similar to rescue dogs, need to be physically agile to reach all kinds of possible hiding places and it is not at all unusual for a Spaniel to be employed in such an operation, due to the breed's physical suppleness which enabling them to wriggle through to enclosed hiding places.

Training methods for Explosives Detection Dogs are generally identical to those for a Drug Detection Dog, except that the dog is taught to search for explosives and not drugs.

Every explosive has its own olfactory component, and each component belongs to the family of 'aromatic nitrocomposites'. The dog is trained to identify the following single components: TNT, Tetryl, foil explosives, Amongelite, Nitroglycol, Seismo-Gelite, Nitropenta, Hexogen, Nitrocellulose, gunpowder, Fle-X, Semtex and PETN.

One facet of Explosives Detection training is different from that of Drug Detection training. The instinct of a Drugs Detection Dog is aroused by the use of a plastic retrievable toy, which he scratches after having found the desired drugs. However, such scratching could cause the early death of an Explosives Detection Dog, or perhaps an even worse catastrophe. The modified training requires that the dog shows the location of the explosives by assuming the Down position, or by barking from a distance.

An Explosives Detection Dog's work is extremely dangerous, and everything must be done to ensure that no boring routine develops. Unfortunately, modern society has brought with it dangers arising from visits by high-ranking politicians and guests of the State. It has become mandatory to carefully check entire venues, including banquet halls, hotel rooms, embassies and other government accommodation, to rule out the presence of explosives.

These dogs have prevented catastrophes and saved people's lives. They have become an important instrument in the protection of human life. As I mentioned earlier, the responsibilities of Drug Detection Dogs and Explosives Detection Dogs are still relatively new, but extremely important. These dogs are doing us a great service; some Explosives Detection Dogs have paid with their lives while doing their duty on our behalf.

TRACKING DOGS

Any owner who has successfully guided his dog through the trials for a tracking dog knows what dogs can achieve with their noses. Just imagine, a tracklayer takes off in an open field, laying a zig-zagging trail over varying terrain and 'losing' many different items. Only after a wait of three hours are you and your dog allowed to follow the trail, irrespective of any superficial difficulties and in fair weather or foul. The dog handler often starts asking himself if maybe his dog is 'fantasising' and has, in reality, lost the trail. What joy when the dog actually finds the 'missing' items and works the trail to the finish!

Tracking doesn't have the high profile that it used to have, when dogs, as part of a police operation, tracked down a fugitive, thus playing an active role in fighting crime. Today, tracking is a canine sport, providing a competition that is very rewarding. The only minus point is that open countryside suitable for tracking (and on which landowners allow such events to take place) is becoming harder and harder to find. A talent for diplomacy is sometimes needed to allow you and your dog to train satisfactorily. Almost any dog owner with any breed can participate in this canine sport. It doesn't have to be the most difficult of Tracking Dog Trials; working one's own trail for hidden objects can really be a lot of fun.

Let me make a very important comment at this point: knowledge gained from modern behavioural research has proven that, in Tracking Dog discipline, the use of force is counterproductive. Emphasis should always be put on positive reinforcement, in other words, praise for correct behaviour. Canine specialist Thomas Baumann judges from his standpoint as a police dog trainer: "Force causes conflicts. It must be clearly understood that conflict behaviour grows in proportion to the intensity of force."

In the forefront of today's Tracking Dog training methods stands the strengthening of inherent instincts. The desired tracking goal (prey or food) is rewarded only by tracking the trail with precision.

Allow me to repeat; the working Tracking Dog, on his owner's own trail as well as on an unknown trail, gains an ever-changing experience of joint success, strengthening trust for one another in the man/dog team. The pinnacle of such teamwork can be found in the following report on the successful use of Rescue Dogs and Avalanche Dogs, but even when your goals are more modest, Tracking Dog sport is a hugely interesting leisure time hobby!

RESCUE DOGS AND AVALANCHE DOGS

On December 7th 1988, there was an earthquake in the Soviet republic of Armenia. About 100,000 people were caught unprepared by this disaster, and tens of thousands perished under the rubble of their collapsed homes. On December 9th, fourteen Canine Rescue Teams took off from Frankfurt Airport. Here is a short excerpt from a report by Angela Wegmann:

"It's cold, minus 10-15 degrees Celsius, accommodation is in tents, we warm ourselves at an open fire. The dogs sleep closely snuggled next to their handlers during the short pauses throughout the night. The searching work in a stone desert is feverishly continued. People could still be alive under the rubble, they still could be saved. The physical burden on the dog handlers and their animals is enormous The numbers of the missing extend into thousands. Where can one begin? And then come the worst moments for every Rescue Dog handler. A dog searches, already somewhat tired, in the wreckage. His handler is depressed. For days we have only been able to find corpses. All of a sudden, the dog stands riveted to the spot. Checking to make sure, he sticks his nose into a narrow slit under an iron beam. His body stiffens. Joyfully he begins to wag his tail and immediately afterwards beings to bark strongly into the depths. Stress, chaos, over-fatigue are forgotten. The handler recognises immediately that somewhere here under the rubble, someone must still be alive What happens then can be dryly read later in the operations report: 'Unfortunately, the victim could not be rescued due to technical reasons.'

"The dogs don't want to leave the piles of rubble. Areas are marked and shown to the rescue troops. Certainty exists only on the next day. This time their help didn't come too late. A father shows them one of the little shoes from a rescued child, they cannot understand what he is saying. Many people, some here in Armenia, owe their lives to Rescue Dog Teams from all over the world bringing them help when they would have been hopelessly buried alive, because they weren't found in time. Even in this computer age, the canine nose is still the fastest and most accurate locating device."

Let's take a big detour. On the nights of August 16th-17th 1999, the earth shook in western Turkey and, by the night of August 18th, eight rescue teams from Austria were on their way to the disaster area. Twelve Austrian canine handlers, three of whom were women, rendered assistance with their rubble-searching dogs.

I shall quote Herbert Fragner, the Federal Operations director:

"Our area of operation was in the city of Yalova in southwestern Turkey. The damaged area was once a six-storey apartment building that now had been reduced to one storey of rubble. My first impression, as operations director, and that of the other dog handlers, was depressing. People tried to knock holes and entrances into the cement covering. The dog handlers observed their dogs' behaviour with the highest concentration, in order to correctly interpret any sign signalling life. Moreover, the many finds of corpses were also frustrating for us, as we had flown over to rescue as many living people as possible. However, despite the adverse conditions, we can still remember six living people that could be saved. These individuals were found by our group's Rescue Dogs and were actually rescued alive after several hours."

Is it not amazing how many dog lovers all over the world

sacrifice a large amount of their free time to carefully train their dogs for an operation in disaster areas such as these? They know that only a few will have any real opportunity to be employed in an emergency situation. They also know that many of the opportunities to rescue life actually end in finding only corpses, and yet all of these dog owners have freely chosen to prepare their dogs, just in case they are needed in an emergency.

Anyone who has experience of the Working Dog discipline knows that the training of a Rescue Dog requires more time than all of the other canine sport disciplines. Rescue Dog handlers have found in real-life training programmes so much personal reward and have experienced such successes that they stay in readiness for a period of some years. They are prepared to be called up any time a disaster happens in any part of the world where they can help, and there are many too many such disasters!

I admit that numbers of living survivors rescued worldwide have been low, but what really counts in this tremendous effort is that canine rescue teams succeed again and again in saving human lives which could not otherwise have been saved by any other technical device available. I am not one to queue up with empty praise, but I must stress that, together with the training of Dogs for the Disabled, Rescue Dogs' work is certainly one of the noblest and most necessary responsibilities that we dog owners can offer to our fellow citizens.

However, let's not think just of earthquakes and collapsed houses, tunnel cave-ins and other catastrophes where Rescue Dogs are needed on the job. Avalanche Dogs are also important as rescuers of victims buried under the snow. In Germany, Austria and Switzerland, experienced relief groups with well-trained dogs at their side, have already saved many people from a freezing grave at the last minute.

The methods of training an Avalanche Dog are the same as for Rescue Dogs. Training is very time-consuming and tiresome. Sometimes, it is necessary for the dogs to be flown to the rescue area by helicopter, due to the mountainous snow-covered terrain, and our dogs deserve respect and acknowledgement from a general public grateful for their heroic achievements.

SECTION IV: THE CHALLENGES

Chapter Fifteen

THE WAY
FORWARD

In this book I have attempted to prove how important dogs are for people and for the pursuit of their leisure-time activities; dogs are assets for children, families, athletes, senior citizens, the handicapped, the sick and the lonely.

Huge upheavals in the structure of society and modern lifestyles, combined with ever-shrinking living space and people's difficulty in adapting to change, has brought about the phenomenon of unwelcome publicity for dogs; this has been, and will continue to be, reinforced by biased media politics.

SOLVING THE PUBLIC IMAGE PROBLEM

The image of canines presented to the public is partly to blame for this turn of events. Those responsible for canine development must voluntarily and decisively contribute to improving the public image of the dog, providing meaningful publicity which reflects the true nature of the canine.

Everyone must recognise the significance of Mankind's oldest housepet. Even after 15,000 years of domestication, the dog remains Man's unchanging and irreplaceable life companion.

Earlier in this book, I have candidly written about developmental errors in canine breeding and sport, pointing out the damage that humans have inflicted on our dogs. But these developmental errors need to be corrected, not just exposed as the object of criticism.

All of the services rendered by dogs to humans – thoroughly discussed in the section entitled *What We Have To Lose* – justify more tolerance and justice towards dog lovers on the part of the general public. Standards shouldn't only be set for how many tons of canine faeces are allowed, or whether dogs bark on purpose to disturb the neighbours, nor legislation be based on the occasional and shocking dog-related incident – all these things can simply be attributed to the residual percentage of danger when people interact with animals.

The newest scientific research cited by Stig Carlson justifies the request continually to support all studies which could quantify and assess the wide fields of activity in which our dogs could be of more help to people. Dogs can, through their intelligence, adaptability and willingness to serve help a variety of people and not just the disabled.

An important step would be to investigate new areas of canine deployment, which should then be intensified and supported more strongly in European countries. Also that current research and planning, encompassing specialities and disciplines, must be developed by working together with behavioural researchers, geneticists and professional veterinarians.

From the standpoint of the European Union's recommendations about the avoidance of 'Qualzuchten' (breeds that suffer due to the extreme physical standards set by breeders), it will be a step forward for those in dog breeding. Such a move will be seen as fulfilling and honouring the (in Germany) newly formulated scientific document of June 2nd 1999, banning 'Qualzuchtungen'. This was compiled by animal protection and domestic animal breeding organisations, who can now actively work together with canine researchers for the benefit of our dogs.

We humans have created our dogs and selected individual breeds to do important tasks for us, thus easing and enriching our lives. In the last hundred years, dogs have primarily been useful by doing their duty, assisting us in hunting, agriculture, protection of life and property and participation in two World Wars, during both of which our dogs paid a heavy price with their lives. Our dogs fulfilled all of these duties serving Man.

Our dogs are still actively serving Man in this new millennium. Think of the work of Rescue and Avalanche Dogs and those helping to fight crime. Explosives Detection Dogs protect us from misguided fanatics and Drug Detection

Dogs find the dangerous drugs that threaten all of our society. Immeasurable aid results from the work of assistance and therapy dogs in ever more numerous and expanding fields of duty, serving the blind and caring for the disabled. All these areas of activity will be increased in the 21st century.

The active integration of dogs into our society is urgently needed so that the development of these services for Man can proceed without delay.

OUR DOGS' REQUIREMENTS OF US
Here are a few thoughts on this subject:

1. Respect for the canine as an independent living creature.
The dog is not a miniature human, nor, emphatically, a Tamagotchi, but a living being with his own senses, instincts and needs. Each case of humanising a dog – even if it is well meant – disturbs the mutual understanding of man for dog and vice versa.

2. Fair maintenance in accordance with the species.
As a prerequisite to help him develop his senses and use all of his positive qualities, a dog must be kept in accordance with his canine nature. Dogs held on a chain, kennelled, banished from rented apartments, forced to wear a muzzle and leash when taken out – all of this diminishes our dogs.

It is the responsibility of local goverment to mediate and find a compromise between the interests of dog owners and those of their fellow citizens. Open areas must also be created in our cities, where well-behved dogs are permitted to move about freely. It should also be an important public responsibility to provide canine instructional centres with fenced-in areas where young or behaviourally disturbed animals can learn to behave in public without causing a disturbance and also learn how to adapt to our environment. Canine sports centres should be established and supported, where our four-legged companions can have the chance to work off the surplus energy that can sometimes build up due to urban environmental conditions.

3. Protection from lawmakers.
It is absolutely intolerable that in broad areas of our legal system the canine is still viewed, and dealt with, as an object. This stems from an old-fashioned attitude, one did not recognise the elevated position of the dog as a living being, in comparison to that of a static object. In principle, this requirement is extended to cover all animals! The adoption of animal protection as a funadamental right is urgently needed as part of the constitution.

4. Protection against abuse.
The adoption of animal protection in the constitution would certainly be an important step towards the protection of pitiful laboratory dogs. It would considerable reduce the number of abused animals, and abolish the priority that science and research is given when it comes to animal protection. Strict policing of commercial dealing in dogs and if possible, a ban on canine trafficking is a necessity. Such an arrangement would much more successfully control public disturbances than the exaggerated discrimination against so-called fighting dogs. Deployment of all legal and law-enforcement means against the abuse of the dog could be a strong weapon, and action against abusive, illegal dog fights is needed. Full deployment of present laws to punish animal abusers, particularly for serious infringements of animal protection laws, should be reinforced by a ban on dog ownership for many years. Finally, carefully balanced domestic animal protection law is urgently needed to keep 'wild canine breeding' under control.

5. The education of our children.
This is a broad area. Starting in kindergarden, our children must have the chance to be liberated from the fears that have been instilled into them by their falsely informed parents. Please note that 90 per cent of all accidents with canines are caused by the incorrect behaviour of the person, not the inherent danger of the animal! Only the continual contact and familiarity with animals for all schoolchildren will improve the situation. Whenever possible this initiative should include direct contact with the animals and so allow youngsters to learn how to behave in their presence.

6. Tolerance and recognition

It is a fact that in our modern society, year after year, more lives are saved by the efforts of dogs than are lost through any incidents involving dogs. The same goes for health issues. We must emphasise the enormous achievement of the canine as companion, children's attendant, and on-the-job carer for the handicapped, sick and aged.

These facts should be publically recognised. It is always an enormous surprise for me to observe how natural it is in the UK to grant such public recognition, and how difficult this unfortunately seems to be for those in German-speaking countries.

So that these demands not be misinterpreted, my call for tolerance for dogs should not be viewed as one-sided. Any demand for tolerance must always be bound up with an understanding of the feelings of others. I admit that tolerance is not a necessarily a prevalent quality in all dog owners – many disturbances are created by the dog owners thenselves. What is required is a responsible, strict self-examination on both sides of the dog debate!

But one last thing should be highlighted at the end of this book – the dog as a living being. Man's oldest domestic animal is entitled to his own rights in our society, providing us, as he does, with services that are urgently needed by people in the 21st century. For all these reasons, I believe the dog deserves complete recognition, great respect and careful protection!